AISU KAGE RYU

愛洲陰之流

THE SHADOW SCHOOL OF SWORD

:

DOCUMENTS FROM 1561 ~ 1865

AISU IKOSAI

Table of Contents

1	Introduction	6
2	Origin of the Shadow School Through Documents	9
3	Scroll 1 Leaping Monkey Catalogue	29
4	Scroll 2 The Mountain Goblin Scroll	63
5	Scroll 3 The Dueling Sword Scroll	101
6	Scroll 4 Blindfolded Scroll	123
7	Other Shadow School Documents	130

Wakou Pirates & The Shadow School
16th & 17th Century Chinese Military Manuals

8	Translator's Introduction	209
9	Song of the Japanese Sword (1) By Ouyang Xiu (1007 ~ 1072)	210
10	Song of the Japanese Sword (2)	214
11	New Words from Guangdong	220
12	Excerpts from: New Treatise on Military Efficiency	223
13	Excerpts from: Bubishi	239
14	Tales of the Foreign Country Known as Japan	262
15	Excerpts from: The Japanese Pirate Sword	274

Introduction to The Aisu Shadow School

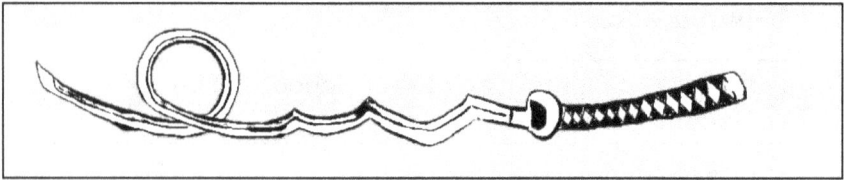

Overview

Aisu Kage Ryu, The Aisu Shadow School of Sword, was founded by Aisu Iko, whose full name is Ikosai Hisatada 愛洲移香斎久忠 (1452-1537.) The Shadow School is considered to be one of the "Three Great Schools of Sword Fighting" along with the Shinto School and Nen School. Aisu is possibly a grandson of Saru no Gozen, who was one of the 14 original disciples of the founder of Nenryu, Nenami Jion 念阿弥慈恩 who lived in the 14th century. The Aisu family may have been Wakou (Japanese pirates) who raided the Korean and Chinese coastal cities.

Aisu develop the Shadow School sometime in the Choho Era (1487-1489) when he was around 37 years old. He began a period of introspection in a cave at Udo Temple in Kyushu. While in the stone chamber he received divine inspiration from a supernatural being that revealed the inner mysteries of the sword. Some stories say it was an old man who had taken the form of a spider, others say it was a monkey that taught him to train against his own shadow. In Japanese the word *Kage* means shadow, though it can also refer to the Yin (of Yin and Yang.) Aisu Iko considered sword techniques to be Yin, or the obverse, and your spirit to be Yang, the reverse.

The Shadow School of Sword began to spread all over Kyushu and was used by the Wakou Japanese pirates that prowled the waters around the Korean Peninsula and the shores of southeastern China. The weapons and tactics used by the pirates were so effective the Chinese generals scrambled to find a defense. Later, after capturing a Shadow School document from pirates, the information was reproduced in Chinese military manuals. The manuals included information on the dimensions of Japanese swords, descriptions of techniques and illustrations of sword stances. Later volumes included an illustrated guide and a training manual.

Aisu Iko's heir was Aisu Koshiro Munemichi. Koshiro spread the Shadow School to eastern Japan and taught the art to Kamiizumi Hidetsuna, who founded the New Shadow School. In turn, Kamiizumi taught Yagyu Munenori who founded the Yagyu New Shadow School. Eventually members of the Yagyu New Shadow School became the official sword instructors to the Togugawa Shogun.

The primary goal of this book was to translate the four Aisu Kage "Shadow" School documents that contain pictures of Tengu. Tengu are a kind of mountain goblin that alternate between trickster and helpful teacher of marital arts. I realized that many other Kage "Shadow" School, and later New Shadow School documents used Tengu, so I decided to follow those documents through time. This search ended up including several Chinese sources, due to the curious fact that Japanese Wakou pirates, who pillaged the eastern coast of China in the 16th century, were versed in Shadow School sword fighting. This is evidenced by a document seized by the Chinese and later included in several martial arts manuals.

General Seki Keiko 戚繼光 (1528~1588), who called for subjugation of the Wakou pirate menace, captured a partial copy of the Kage School document in 1561. He had copy made of the seized Japanese document and included it in the 1584 edition of *New Treatise on Military Efficiency* 紀效新書. In 1614 a Chinese man named Cheng Zongyou 程宗猷 (1561-1636) wrote an illustrated book on how to use the Japanese long sword called *Selected Techniques with the Japanese Single Edged Sword* or *The Japanese Pirate Sword* 單刀法選.

Later, in 1621 Bo Genki 茅元儀 (1594~1640) had the illustrations related to the Shadow School reprinted in *New Treatise on Military Efficiency* re-done and included in his 240 volume military manual *The Bubishi* 武備志[1].

---

[1] This book is also known as *Treatise on Armament Technology.*

Origin of the Shadow School Through Documents

Origin of the Shadow School Through Documents
Translator's Introduction

There is a lot of conflicting information regarding the founder of the Shadow School, it's development and evolution into the New Shadow School. The following excerpts are from contemporary scholarship and Densho (historical documents of transmission) highlight some of the discrepancies and difficulties surrounding researching this school.

新影流

凡兵法者亘梵漢和三国有之於
梵者七仏師文殊三持之摂護智
恵剣截断無明賊一切衆生莫
不懼其刃可謂兵法濫觴摩
利支尊天専以為妙術者也於
漢者三皇昔黄帝従反泉涿鹿
而下泛五帝三王元明不断
絶者兵法也於倭自伊弉諾尊
伊弉冊尊至今日不可一日無之
其中有影流之外不儻斗為尭古
奥源荒彩流於抽於奇妙等
妙流平不飛流漾小速法定
浮魚急釜玄中鈴呈法漾自
若魚平期中人英彙徐志平
傳予家法古人豈不通深流剣

二、永禄九年（一五六六）五月、上泉伊勢守秀綱改め信
綱が柳生新左衛門尉に伝えた目録の第一。

新　影　流

凡兵法者、亘二梵漢和
三国一有レ之、於レ梵者、七
仏師、文殊上将提レ持
智恵剣、截二断無明賊一、
則一切衆生莫レ不レ懼二
其刃一可レ謂二兵法濫觴一、
摩利支尊天専以為二
妙術一者也、於レ漢者、三皇
昔、黄帝従レ勝二反泉涿
鹿一、而下自二五帝三王一
至二元明一不レ断絶レ者兵法
也、於レ倭者、自二伊弉諾
尊、伊弉冊尊、至二今日一、
不レ可二一日無一之其中

Shin Kage School[2]

All of martial arts ordinates from three countries India, China and Japan. From India we have the Seven Incarnations of the Buddha and Manjushree (the Bodhisattva that represents transcendent wisdom). By raising the sword of wisdom they can cut/ pass judgement on the unenlightened villains and separate them from all living things.

There was no area untouched by that blade and it can be said to be the origin of Heiho, martial arts and sword fighting. Marishïten became the sole possessor of secret teachings. Long ago (26th century BC,) during the reign of Three Sovereigns, the Yellow Emperor defeated Chiyou at the Battle of Zhuolu 涿鹿 之戰. The sword fighting techniques used in that battle have been handed down unbroken from the reign of the Three Sovereigns and The Five Emperors (circa 2852 BC to 2070 BC) to Empress Genmei 元明天皇(660 – 721.)

In Japan we have the omnipresent deities the glorious Izanagi and the glorious Izanami, who married and gave birth to the islands of Japan as well as other gods.

Later the oldest schools were formed. Chuko Nenryu (Middle Old Nen School) Shinto School and Kage School. There are innumerable other schools.

---

[2] This is a 1566 document written by Kami Izumi Nobutsuna to Yagu Munenori.

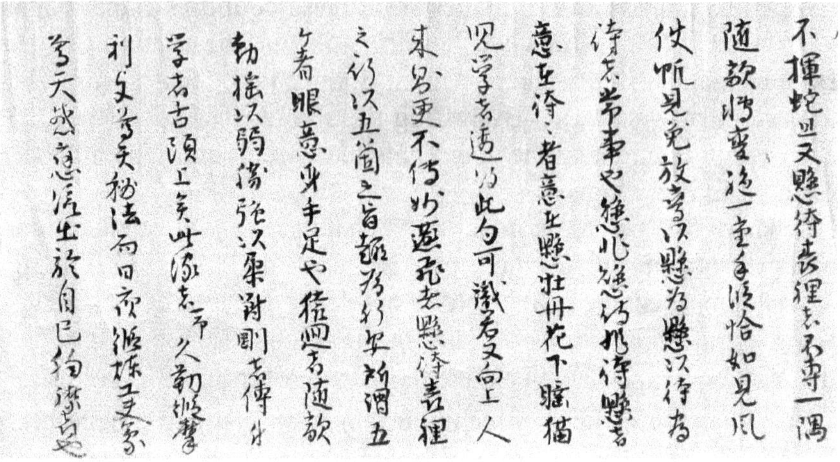

間、有ニ上古流、中古念
流・新当流ニ亦復有
陰流其外不勝計、予
究ニ諸流奥源一於ニ陰流ニ
別抽ニ出奇妙一号ニ新陰
流一、予不レ廃ニ諸流一而不レ
認ニ諸流ニ、寔得レ魚忘レ
筌者乎、然則諸流位、
別莫耳、非ニ千人英、万
人傑一争伝ニ予家法一
古人豈不レ道、誅竜
剣不レ揮レ蛇、且又懸
得表裡者不レ守ニ二
隅一随レ敵転変、施ニ二重
手段一恰如レ見ニ風使レ帆
見レ兎放レ鷂以レ懸為レ
懸、以レ待為レ待者常事
也、懸非レ懸、待非レ待、懸

I studied Kage School, which is comprised of the inner mysteries of all other sword schools. Having mastered it, I was able to distill an even greater mystery from my training and called this new creation Shin Kage Ryu, The New Shadow School.

I have in no way abandoned all other schools while at the same time I do not submit myself to other schools. The truth is that the techniques you learn should be removed from your active memory, like forgetting the cylindrical bamboo fishing basket once you have caught the fish. I do not place the schools of war in any hierarchy.

I will not teach my art to anyone whose bravery does not exceed that of a thousand of his fellows and 10,000 average men. As an old teacher once said,

Don't pass to a snake the sword you used to kill a dragon

I want to emphasize that you do not become fixated on only one aspect strategy, whether it is waiting for the enemy to attack or making the first move. This also applies to any variation therein either using a strategy of appearing to wait or a strategy of appearing to be ready to make the first attack.

You should move according to the enemy's variations, taking only as much action as necessary. This is like judging the wind when setting your sail or watching a rabbit before releasing your hawk. Attacking first means completely committing to attacking first, waiting for the enemy to attack first means completely committing to waiting for that attack.

It is not attacking first in order to attack, it is not waiting for the attack for the sake of waiting. Attacking first can also mean waiting for the enemy to attack. Waiting for the enemy to attack can also mean attacking first.

者意在レ待、待者意
在レ懸、牡丹花下睡猫
児、学者、透ニ得此句
可レ識、若又向上人束、
則更施ニ不伝妙一、

燕飛者懸待表裡之行、以ニ
五箇之旨趣一為ニ簡要一、所
謂五ヶ者眼・意・身・手・足也、
猿廻者随レ敵動揺、以レ弱勝レ強
以レ柔制レ剛者、伝ニ付学
者ニ舌頭上矣、此流者、予
久日勤ニ修摩利支
尊天秘法一而日夜鍛
煉工夫、蒙ニ尊天感
応一忽然而流一出於自己一
胸襟ー者也、

山陰（燕飛太刀第三）

月影（同四）

浦波（同五）

浮舟（同六）

獅子奮迅（燕飛太刀附随の極意太刀）

山霞（同前）

上州之住人

　　上泉伊勢守

　　　藤原信綱（印、花押）

永禄九丙寅五月吉日

It is necessary to understand the meaning of the famous saying, *The sleeping kitten under the peony flowers.* While the kitten may appear to be napping, if someone approaches it, the kitten will run off. Only if the Buddhist monk Shunjo 俊聖 (1239 - 1287) appeared could you receive a greater mystery never revealed to others.

Enpi, Flying Kite (Shin Kage School changed the initial Kanji from monkey to Kite), is the epitome of the interchangeable duality of Attacking First and Waiting to Attack. There are five essential focus points in this technique. To put them simply the five points are the eyes, your intent, your body, your hands and your feet.

Enkai, Revolving Monkey, means to move as the enemy necessitates, showing weakness before defeating strength. Controlling the enemy's rigidity with your flexibility is what I wish to transmit to anyone learning this technique. I have devoted innumerable days studying the secrets the great Marishiten wove into this school.

Day and night I forged my body and mind as I developed new ways of training to find new insights. I received sudden divine insight from Marishiten and took it to heart before passing letting it flow into you.

A Resident of Joshu 上州之住人
Kamiizumi Ise no Kami 上泉伊勢守
Fujiwara Nobutsuna 藤原信綱
Official Kao Seal 花押
An Auspicious Day in Genroku 9 永録九年五月吉日 (1566)

新陰流紅葉観念の巻
Shinkageryu Koyo Kannen no Maki
New Shadow School: How to Look at the Fall Colors Scroll
Edo Era

Fuxi 伏羲[3] was once fishing and pulled a turtle up from the bottom of the ocean he marked it with the eight characters of the Hakke 八卦[4] and was able to divine good and evil from the heavens. Martial arts were revealed to him and these were used in order to stabilize the world.

---

[3] A legendary Chinese hero. He and his sister/wife Nüwa with created humanity, music, hunting, fishing, as well as writing around 2,000 BC

[4] Bagua: eight symbols used in Taoist cosmology to represent the fundamental principles of reality.

Udo Shrine's Gongen: *Ugayafukiaezu no Mikoto* 鵜茸草茸不合命
The father of Japan's first Emperor, Emperor Jimmu.

新陰流解
Shinkageryu Kai
An Explanation of the New Shadow School
Edo Era
Shinkage Ryu

This Kage no Kenpo, Shadow Way of the Sword, was transmitted to the deity Gongen of Udo in Huga Domain.[5] This was in the Reiki Era 霊亀 (715 ~ 717.) From that time on the name of this school was read Japanese-style, which is why it is called Kage no Kenpo, The Shadow Way of the Sword.

However, this Kage no Kenpo, Shadow Way of the Sword, has gone extinct with no trace of it exists any longer. However, in the Onin Era 応仁 (1467~1469), a priest serving the Gongen at the temple named Aisu Iko Fujiwara sought to learn Kage no Kenpo. He withdrew for 17 days inside the shrine and he received a divine response to his prayer, and was enlightened to the inner mysteries of the Shadow Way of the Sword.

Aisu Iko then trained rigorously and further refined the methodology until he had developed new insights. Thus it is recorded that he named his school Shin Kageryu, the New Shadow School.

---

[5] A Gongen is a Buddhist Deity that manifests as a Shinto Deity.

当流由来の巻
Toryu Yurai no Maki
A Scroll on the Origin of This School
By Kamiizumi Guardian of Musashi
Edo Era

<u>Entry for Aisu Iko</u>

The fundamentals of this school are by a man named Aisu Ikko. He was a master of every sword art and from that base of knowledge he crafted a new school. Aisu's teachings soon spread all over the country. He later made his way to Kyushu where he decided to enter a spiritual place. This was known as the Journey to Udo Cave.

Iko secluded himself in that place for 37 days. He received transmission of this school of sword from the heavens.

新陰流
Shinkage Ryu Yuishu
Origin and History of The New Shadow School
Edo Era

Shinkage Ryu

This school is called Shinkage Ryu, the New Shadow School. It contains all the sword strategies developed by (Yagyu) Muneyoshi after a long span of intense Kenjutsu training. One day it came to pass that Muneyoshi had a duel with his teacher the Guardian of Musashi (Kamiizumi Tsunehisa.)
Kamiizumi startled Muneyoshi by declaring,

You have thoroughly absorbed all my lessons and even surpassed them to the point you have won. It is no exaggeration to say that your skill is hardly that of an average man. Further, it seems equivalent to that of Marishiten. You have become my teacher. Therefore I believe you have renewed this art.

Due to this the name was changed from Kage Ryu, the Shadow School, to Shinkage Ryu, the New Shadow School.

Thus according to the above passage, it was Yagyu Muneyoshi who first used the name "New Shadow School." However, the consensus is that Kamiizumi Guardian of Musashi took the teachings of Aisu Iko and refined them. His school, Shinkage Ryu, was a refinement of Aisu Iko's Kage Ryu, which can now be thought of as Kokage Ryu, Old Shadow School.

甲陽軍鑑
Koyo Gunkan
Record of the Military Exploits of the Takeda Clan
Attributed to Kōsaka Masanobu 高坂 昌信
Edo Era

Kamiizumi Guardian of Ise

Miwa Castle fell in the 6th year of Eiroku. Among the 200 or so mounted Samurai under the command of the Guardian of Mino, a man named Kamiizumi, the Guardian of Ise, acquired a remarkable amount of merit during the siege. He was invited to an audience with general Takeda Shingen, who asked details about him. Kamiizumi responded, I originally studied Aisu Kage no Ryu, Aisu School of the Shadow. I used that knowledge to create Shinkage Ryu.

Kamiizumi added, I am currently preparing to go on Musha Shugyo, a training pilgrimage, around all of Japan. Would Lord Takeda Shingen allow me to do this?

Kamiizumi was granted permission to take leave and embark on his sword pilgrimage instead of serving Lord Takeda directly.

外物武略巻略解

Tonomono Buryaku Maki Ryakukai

A Brief Explanation of Sub-techniques of the New Shadow School

1718

Numerous Secrets of Our School

This is a scroll about Aisu Iko who lived long ago. He was the one who developed the deepest roots of this school, from which everything else grows.

From days long past the Aisu family served the Fujiwara Family, for generation after generation. They worked in the service of Udo Daikongen. In other words they were priests in charge of Udo Shrine, and their family has worked until the present day at the Shrine in Hyuga Domain

During the time Kamiizumi the Guardian of Musashi was alive, Aisu Iko's designated heir was Aisu Koshichiro. He was a well-known swordsman and an honor to the school. Aisu Koshichiro was the man who transmitted the teachings of this school to the Guardian of Musashi. Later his martial arts ability became famous far and wide.

Hikita Bungoro had a Kenjutsu duel with the Guardian of Musashi. Kamiizumi affirmed that Bungoro had without question completed his Shugyo, intensive training, and had achieved his goal with Kenjutsu.

Bungoro later transmitted his knowledge to Ueno Sanosuke who continued the tradition.

師系集傳
Shikeishuden
The Lineage of Japanese Sword Masters
Katoda Hirahachiro 加藤田平八郎
1843

Entry For Aisu Iko

He was born in Oshu during the time when the power of the Ashikaga Shogun was in decline. From a young age he was fond of learning sword and spear techniques. He later embarked on Musha Shugyo, a martial arts pilgrimage, around Japan. He travelled far and wide, eventually ending up in Kyushu. There he secluded himself in a stone chamber in Udo and prayed to discover the subtle mysteries of Kenjutsu.

In a dream, a monkey-god appeared before him and revealed the inner mysteries of the sword arts. Immediately he was flooded with realization and with this great enlightenment he called his school Kage Ryu.

If Aisu Iko did not feel a person was worthy, he would not teach them. Aisu is the founder of Kage Ryu, a newly revitalized method of sword and spear fighting. Kamiizumi Nobutsuna continued to teach this school.

剣道の発達
Kendo no Hattatsu
The Development of Kendo
Shimokawa Ushio 下川潮
1925

In the Warring States period the use of Kanji was a jumble. Writers all had their own way of using Kanji. They had no qualms about using a different Kanji to write a word as long as it had the same pronunciation or meaning. In addition, writers would have no qualms about using alternate versions of kanji. These could be older Kanji not used in Japan or Kokuji, Kanji created in Japan.

Some examples are how to write Shinkage Ryu:

新陰流 New + Shadow + School
新影流 New + Shadow (alternate Kanji for Shadow) + School
神影流 Divine + Shadow + School
真陰流 True + Shadow + School
真影流 True + Shadow (alternate Kanji for Shadow) + School

兵法家伝書-付新陰流兵法目録事
Heihokadensho and the Catalogue of the New Shadow School

Watanabe Ichiro 渡辺一郎著

1985

This is a Kenjutsu School founded by Aisu Iko. It is also known simply as Kage Ryu or Kage no Ryu. Starting in 1487, after the Shadow School was founded by Iko, it began to spread all over Kyushu and even the Japanese pirates that prowled the waters around the Korean Peninsula and the shores of China studied it. The Kenjutsu used by these Wakou Japanese pirates was apparently quite feared in China at the time.

General Seki Keiko 戚繼光, who called for subjugation of the menace, included an edited version of the Kage School Catalogue: Leaping Monkey Scroll in the 1584 *New Treatise on Military Efficiency* 紀效新書. General Seki apparently obtained the scroll in the 40th year of Kasei (1561,) from a captured Japanese pirate and reproduced fragments of it. In the fourth year of Tenkei (1621,) General Bo Genki included the same document in his *Treatise on Armament Technology* 武備志. However, he had the illustrations re-done so the seven pages of the Kage Ryu Catalogue and sword techniques depicted monkeys. This book, known as the Bubishi in Japanese, was commonly available in Japan during the Edo Era.

愛洲陰之流
Aisu Kage no Ryu
·

Aisu Shadow School
Four Scrolls
1576
Translator's Introduction

Aisu Kage Ryu Scrolls 1576

Scroll 1
Enpi Mokuroku
Leaping Monkey Catalogue
1576

Scroll 2
Tengu no Maki
Tengu Scroll
1576

Scroll 3
Shiai no Tachi
The Dueling Sword Scroll
1576

Scroll 4
Mekakushi
Blindfolded
1576

Translator's Introduction
Overview of the Four Scrolls

The four scrolls are an interrelated set that were granted to a Samurai named Utaki by a Samurai named Yuhara. Here is a general outline of the four scrolls:

Scroll 1 *Enpi Mokuroku* : Leaping Monkey Catalogue

A Mokuroku is a catalogue of techniques and by receiving it a student has been designated to have attained a certain level of proficiency. This scroll contains 11 techniques and begins with Enpi, Leaping Monkey. An earlier version of this scroll fell into the hands of the Chinese navy, who seized it from Wakou Japanese pirates.

Scroll 2 *Tengu no Maki :* Tengu Scroll

The Tengu scroll has very little in the way of explanation. It contains a set of 12 techniques, with a human figure paired with a Tengu. Tengu are mountain goblins that often teach martial arts to to certain worthy students. For the most part the human figures are only armed with a Katana. The Tengu, on the other hand, hold a variety of weapons, including a Naginata (halberd) So-yari (plain spear,) Juji-yari (cross-shaped spear,) two Katana and two Kodachi (short swords.)

Scroll 3 *Shiai no Tachi* : The Dueling Sword

This scroll features humans holding a variety of weapons including Nagamaki, Tachi and Kodachi. There is very little text.

· Scroll 4 *Mekakushi* : Blindfold

This scroll also has a clear title but is clearly an inner secret scroll, likely only given to a practitioner who has achieved a high level.

Scroll 1
愛洲陰之流目録
Aisu Kage no Ryu Mokuroku

・

Enpi Mokuroku
Leaping Monkey Catalogue
1576

Scroll 1
Aisu Kage School Catalogue

可傳　不可傳

但可依弟子

愛洲陰之流目録

Whether you decide to teach this information or not teach this
information all depends on the student.
Aisu Shadow School Catalogue of Techniques

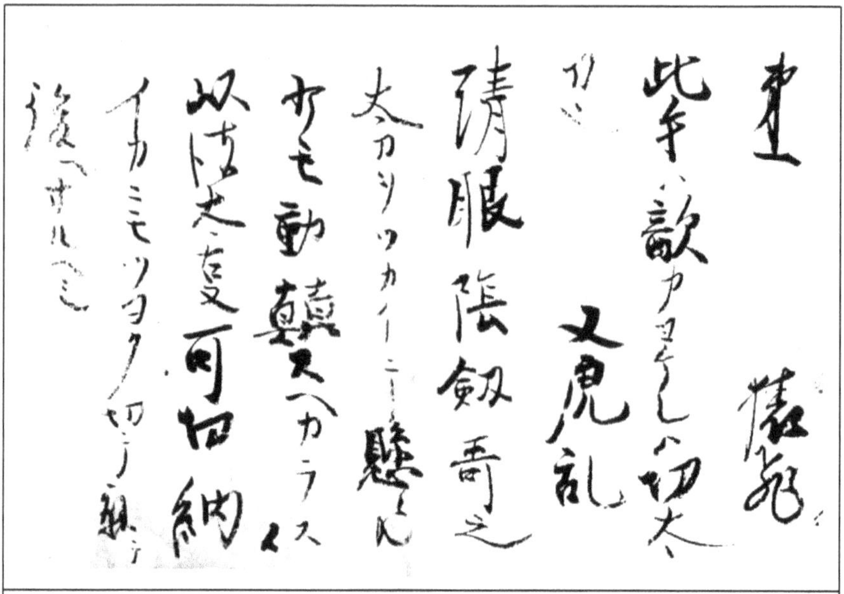

第一　　猿飛

此手ハ敵カヨケレハ切太

刀也　　　又虎乱

清眼　陰劒

太刀ヲツカイテ懸ル心

少モ動顛スベカラス

以傳太事可切納ム

イカニモツヨク切テ懸テ

後ヘサルヘシ

#1 猿飛 *Enpi* Leaping Monkey[6]

If your enemy avoids or blocks your attack, respond with this cut. In addition, this technique can also be used with the following Kamae : *Koran* Wild Tiger, *Seigan* Clear Vision, *Kage Ken* Shadow Sword.

Though you are using your sword to defend, your spirit should maintain the initiative. Do not divert from or allow yourself to be diverted from this strategy.

This is an important lesson and should be thoroughly absorbed. You should take the initiative a cut forcefully, then leap backwards like a monkey[7].

---

[6] "En" is another way to read the Kanji monkey 猿 , which is usually read as "Saru."

[7] The word "Saru" is used. It can mean "to disappear/ depart." It can also mean "monkey." Since the word is not written in Kanji perhaps the writer intended for both meanings to be held at the same time. Therefore "leap backwards like a monkey" uses both meanings, "disappearing" out of range in a simian fashion.

According to the New Yagyu School Secret Scroll 柳生流新秘抄 written in 1716 by Sano Genkatsu 佐野源勝 the meaning of this technique is;
In Enpi you should leap lightly as monkeys do.

In addition;

Your mind should never become fixed on any one thing or you will get caught in the enemy's strategy. That is why this technique is uses the monkey as an example of your mindset

第二　猿廻

此ノ手モ敵切出ス時我太刀
ヲ敵ノ太刀ニ切續テ太刀ヲ
ハツス時切也初之如ク心
得ヘシ

38

#2 猿廻 *Enkai* Circling Monkey

Like the previous technique the attacker cuts at you[8]. You block this with your sword. The moment the swords separate, make your cut.

---

[8] Since this technique starts with "Like the previous technique" we can presume your opponent cuts first in both *Enpi* and *Enkai.*

#3 山陰 *Yamakage* Shadow of the Mountain[9]

---

[9] According to the New Yagyu School Secret Scroll 柳生流新秘抄 the meaning of this technique is;

Shadow of the Mountain is the reverse of Gekkage, Moon and Shadow. It is the Yin-Yang (In-Yo) duality of obverse and reverse, constantly and freely interchangeable.

#4 月陰 *Gekkage* Moon and Shadow[10]

---

[10] The New Yagyu School Secret Scroll 柳生流新秘抄 the meaning of this technique is;

The moon 月 is a shape, and lights up the dark night, shadows 陰 are without shape and are as the dark night. Think of this as "Seeing the shadows by the light of the moon."

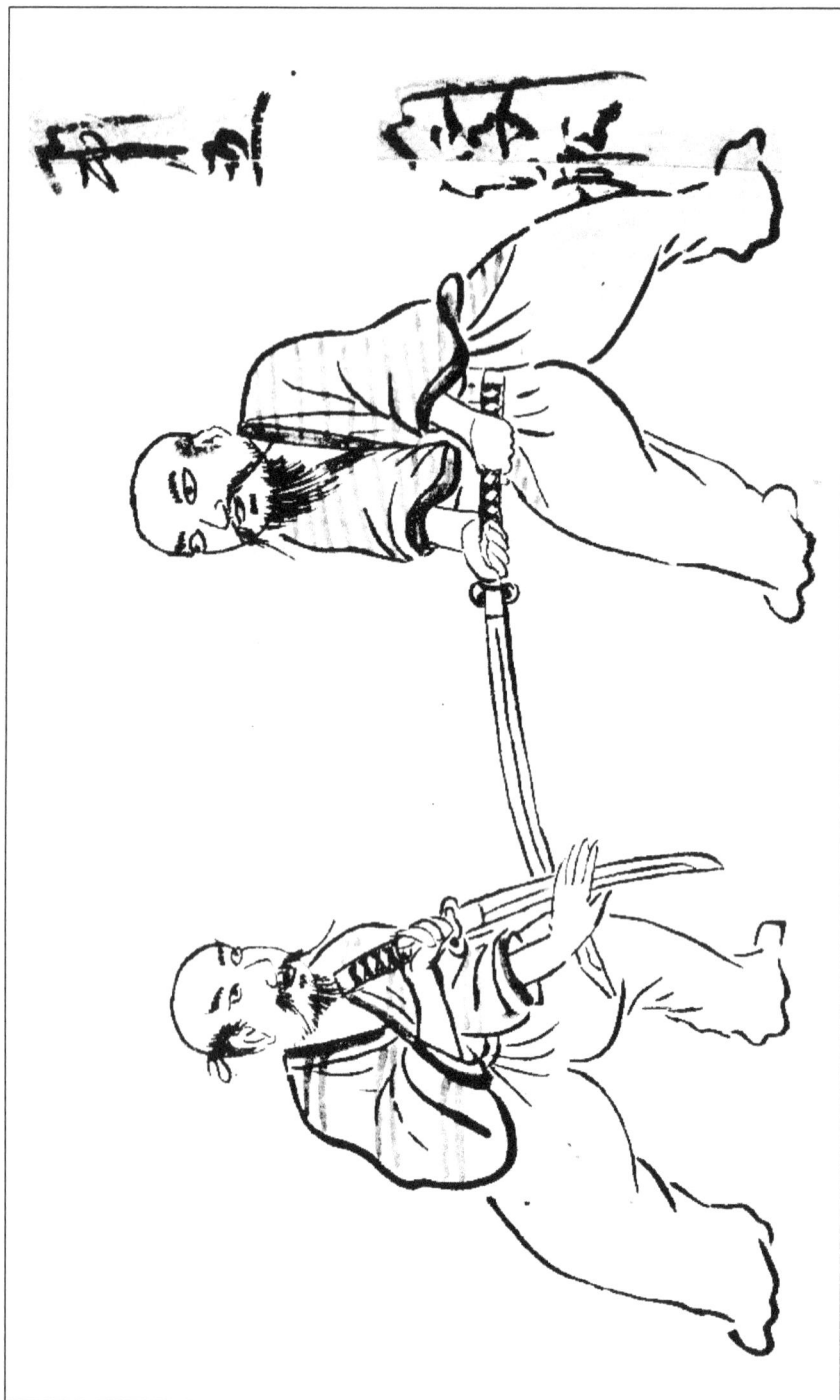

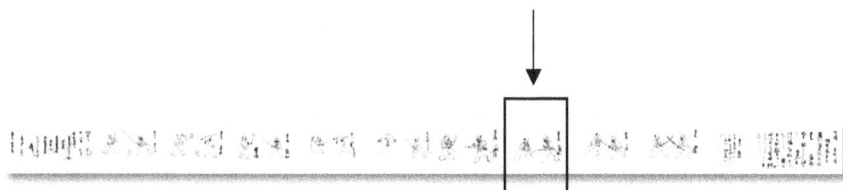

#5 浮舩 *Ukibune* Floating Like a Boat[11]

---

[11] The New Yagyu School Secret Scroll 柳生流新秘抄 the meaning of this technique is;

If you were to strike a hollow gourd floating on water it will quickly just slip away and continue floating.

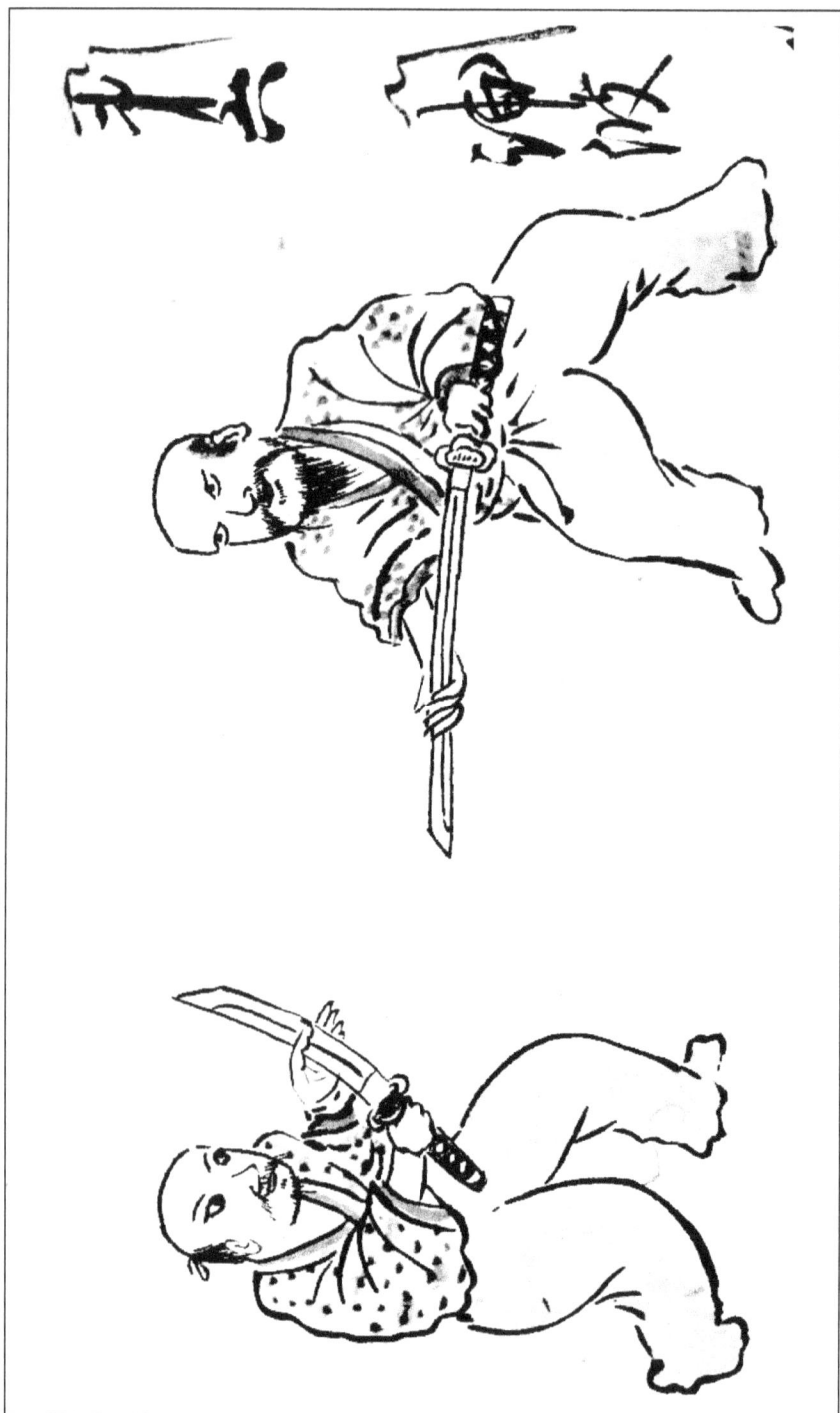

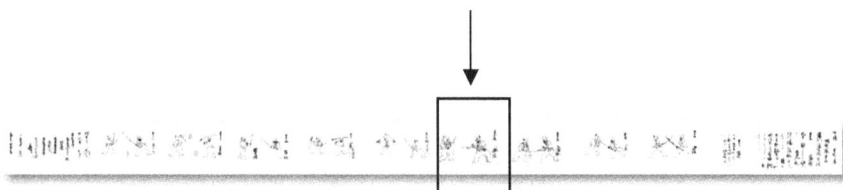

#6 浦波 *Uranami* Returning Wave/ Reversing the Wave[12]

---

[12] The New Yagyu School Secret Scroll 柳生流新秘抄 the meaning of this technique is;

The technique Returning Wave is so named as it should recall a scene where one is gently matching the movement of a wave.

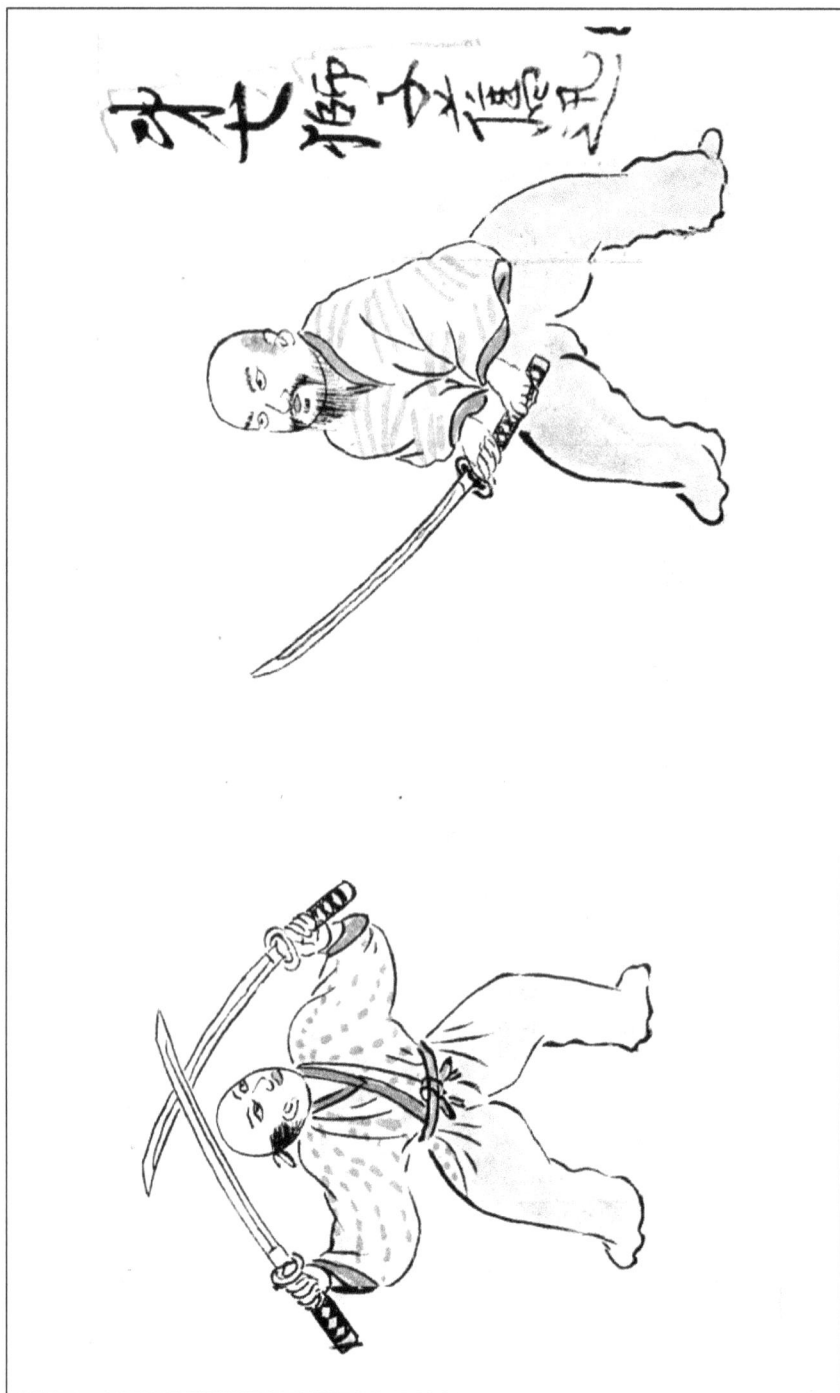

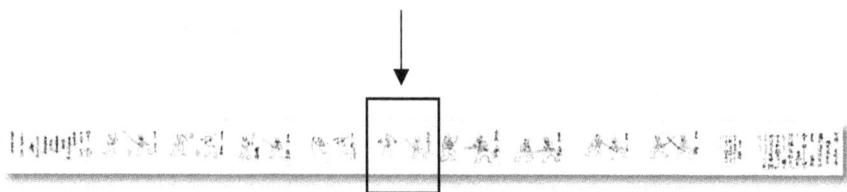

#7 七獅子奮迅 *Shi-Shi-Fun-Jin* An Irresistible Force[13]

---

[13] A more literal translation of this metaphor is "A Wild Tiger Turning to Fight."

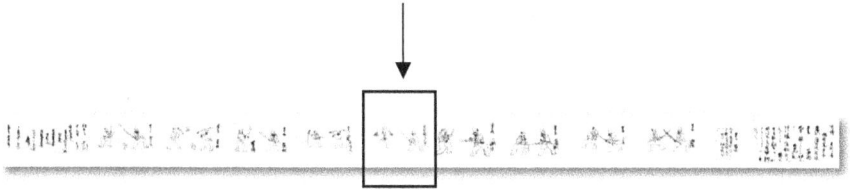

#8 山霞 *Yamakasumi* Mountain Mist[14]
是ハ地具足ニナル心ナリ

You should feel as if armored by the earth.

---

[14] The short notation is very vague. 具足 means armor, however the Kanji for earth 地 is before it. One possibility is this is referring to Kogusoku. 小具足 Kogusoku refers to either armed close combat in light armor or grappling using short edged weapons such as a Wakizashi or a Tanto.

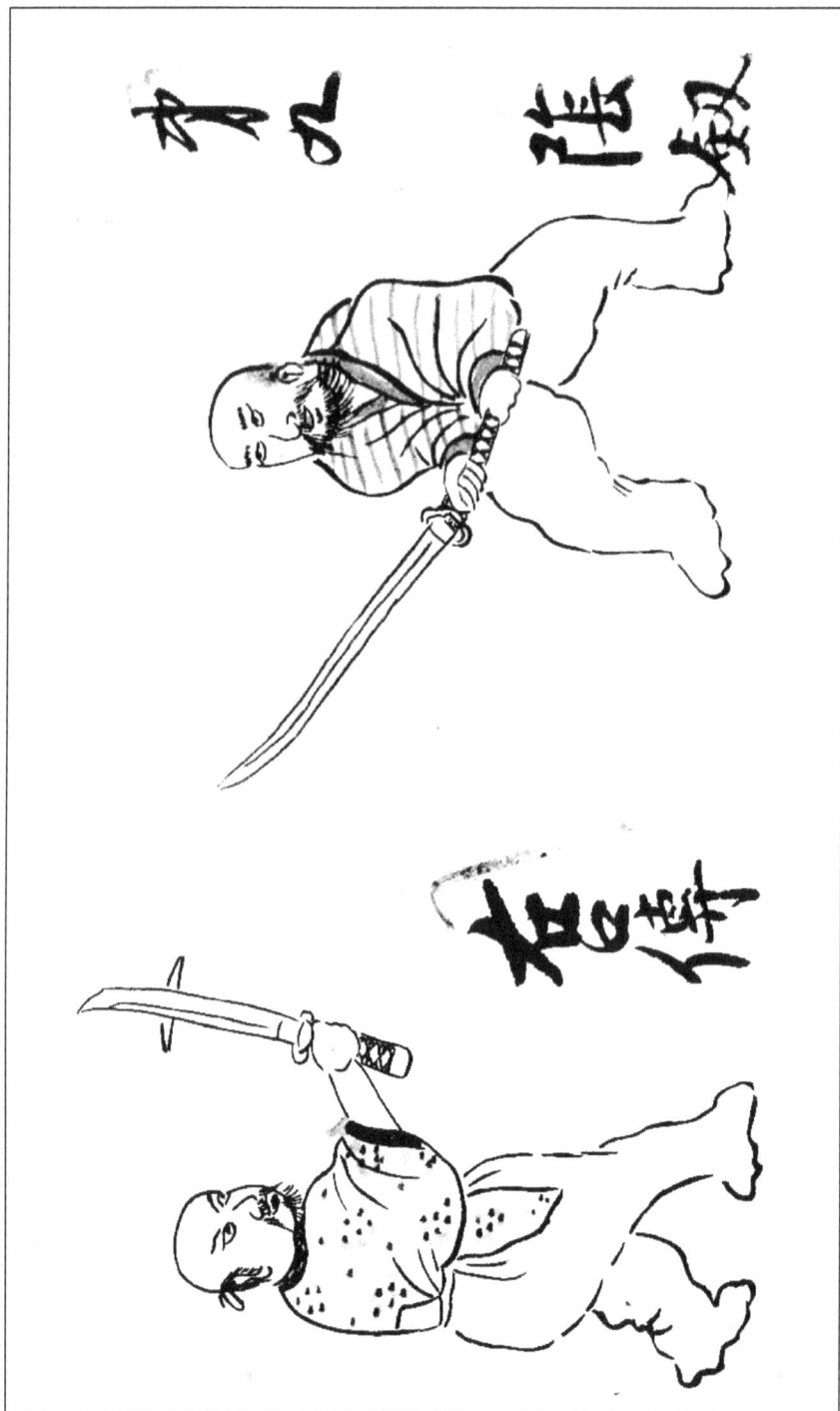

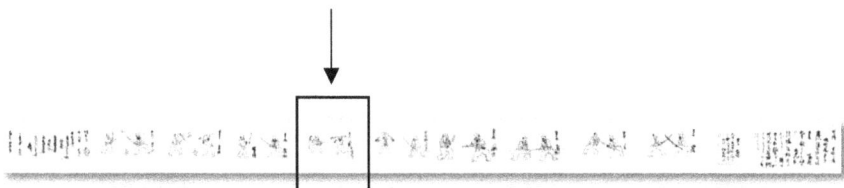

#9 陰劔 *Kage Ken* Shadow Sword
右口傳
There is a Kuden, oral only transmission, about the right.

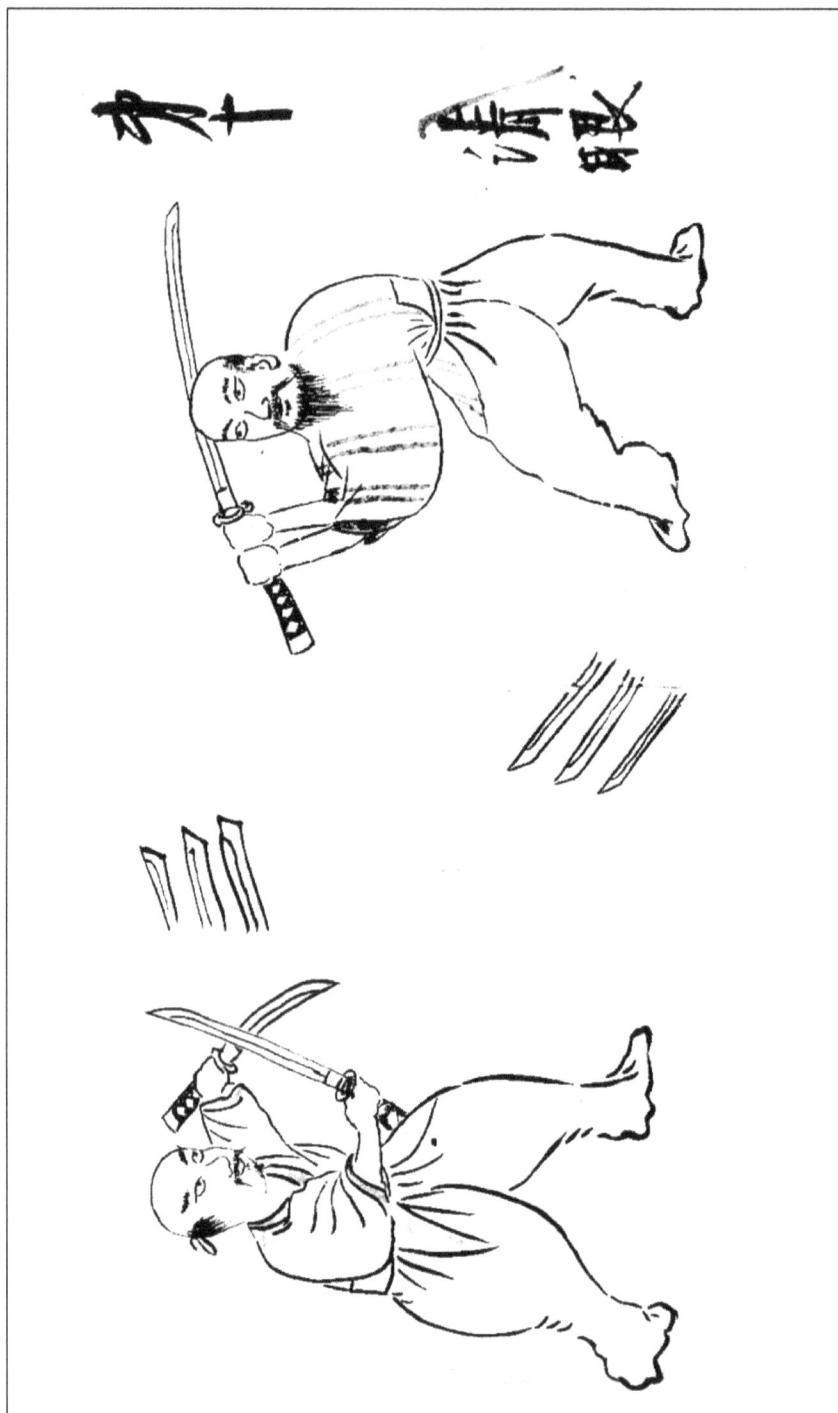

#10 青眼 *Seigan* Clear Eyed

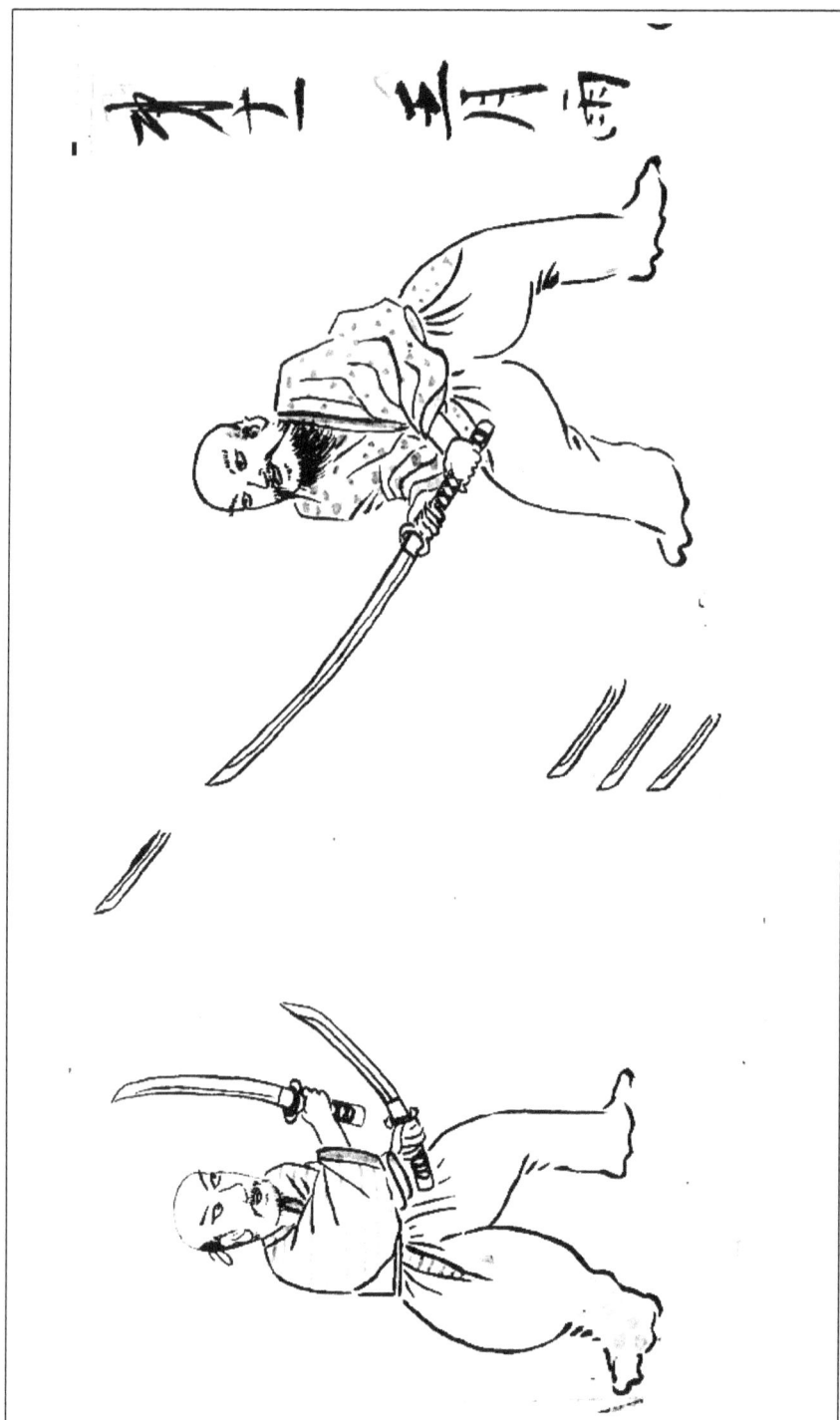

#11 五月雨 *Samidare* Early Summer Rain

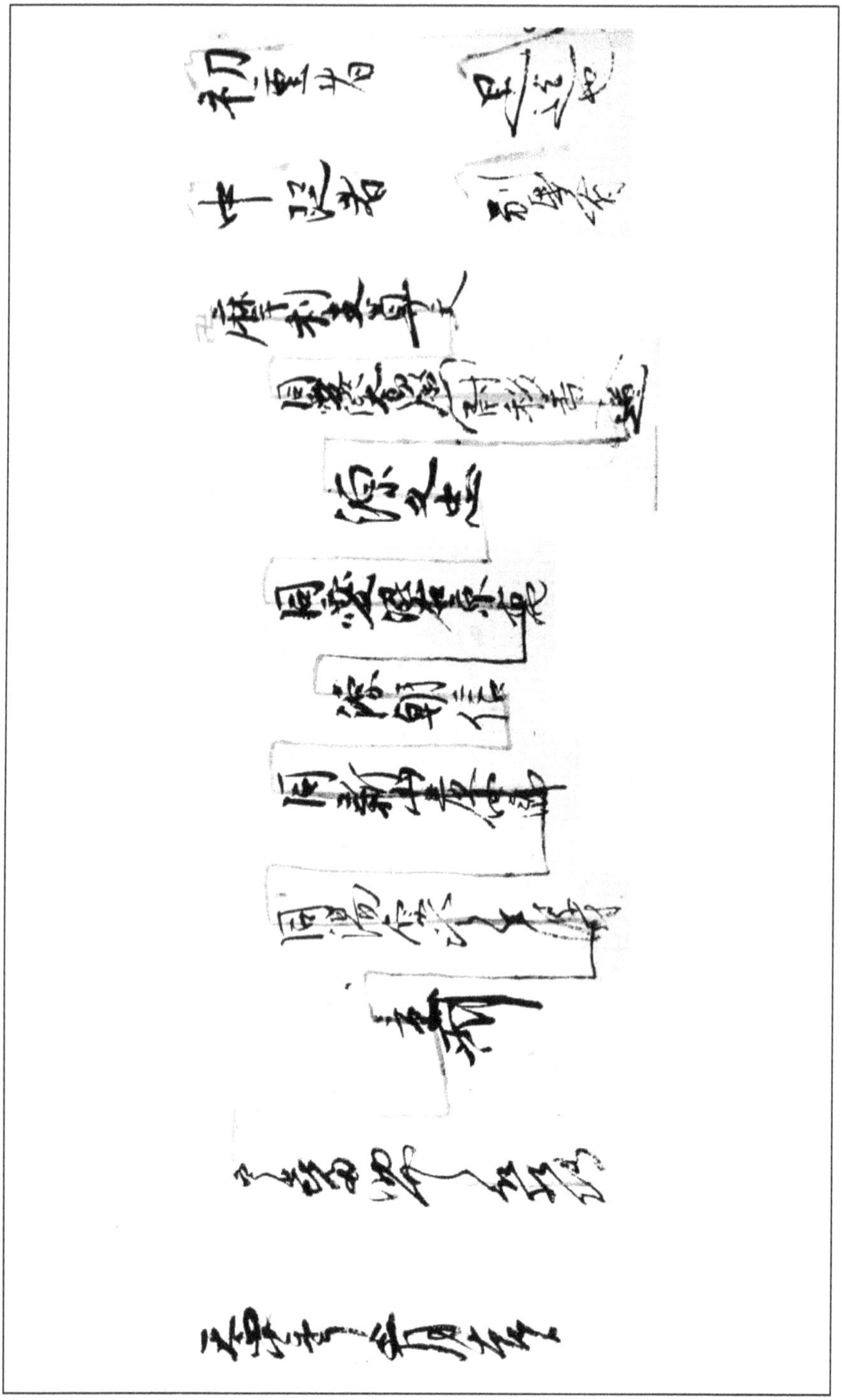

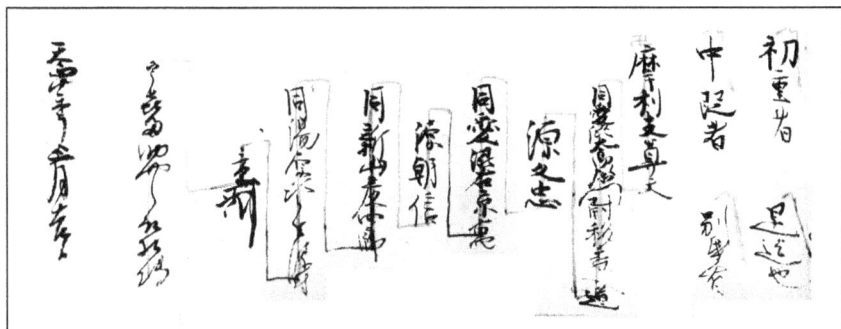

初重者　是迄也

中段者　別紙有

摩利支尊天

同愛洲太郎左衛門尉移香入道

源久忠

同愛洲右京亮

源朝信

同新山彦四郎

同湯原次郎兵衛尉

花押

宇喜多助四郎殿相傳

天正四年三月吉日

初重者　　是迄也
This is the end of the teachings for beginners.
中段者　　別紙有
There is another paper (scroll) for intermediate students.
摩利支尊天
Marishi-Son-Ten[15]
⇩
同愛洲太郎左衛門尉移香入道
Aisu Taro Saemon no Jo Iko Nyudo[16]
⇩
源久忠
Minamoto Hisatada
⇩
同愛洲右京亮
Aisu Ukyuo no Suke
⇩
源朝信
Minamoto Asanobu
⇩
同新山彦四郎
Shinzan Hideshiro
⇩
同湯原次郎兵衛尉
Yuhara Jiro Hyoe no Jo[17]
花押
Kao [18]
宇喜多助四郎殿相傳
Transmitted to Lord Ukita Sukesuke Shiro
天正四年三月吉日
On an auspicious day in March of the 4th year of Tensei 1576

---

[15] The founder of Aisu Kage School is the diety Marishiten. Therefore Ikosai is the "second" head of the school.
[16] Saemon no Jo is his official position in a Domain.
[17] Hyoe no Jo is an official position in a Domain.
[18] A Kao is the artistic signature

Scroll 2

•

Tengu no Maki
Mountain Goblin Scroll
1576

此流之秘密是迄ニテ候

能々被分御覚ヘク候

先之位者心之内有

先如此目録顕候也

This document contains all the secret teachings of this school. You should study this information carefully as you memorize it. This contains all the knowledge of the previous teachers of this school. This is all contained within this Mokuroku Catalogue

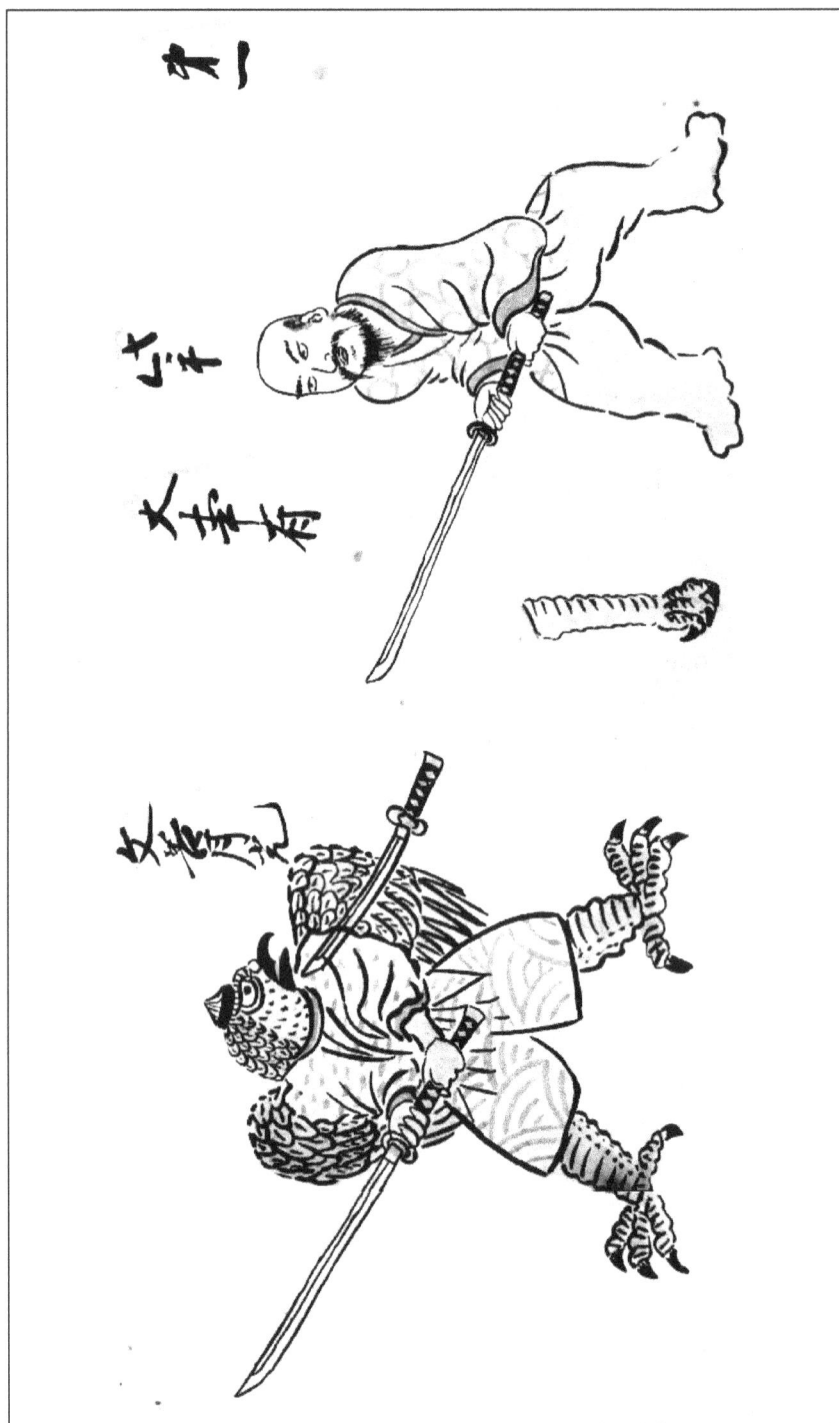

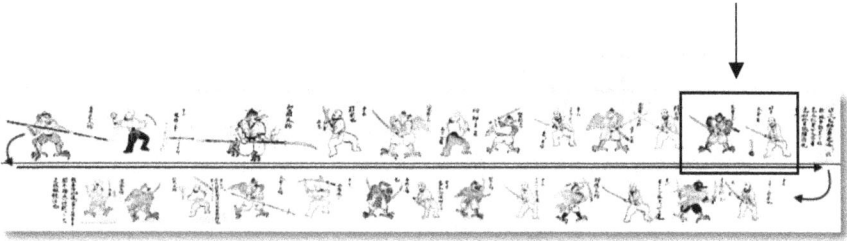

This part of
the technique
is very
important.

第一　文善月光 *Dai Ichi Bunzen Gekko*
此手大事有

Number One: Virtuous Writing by the Light of the Moon Tengu
This part of the technique is very important.

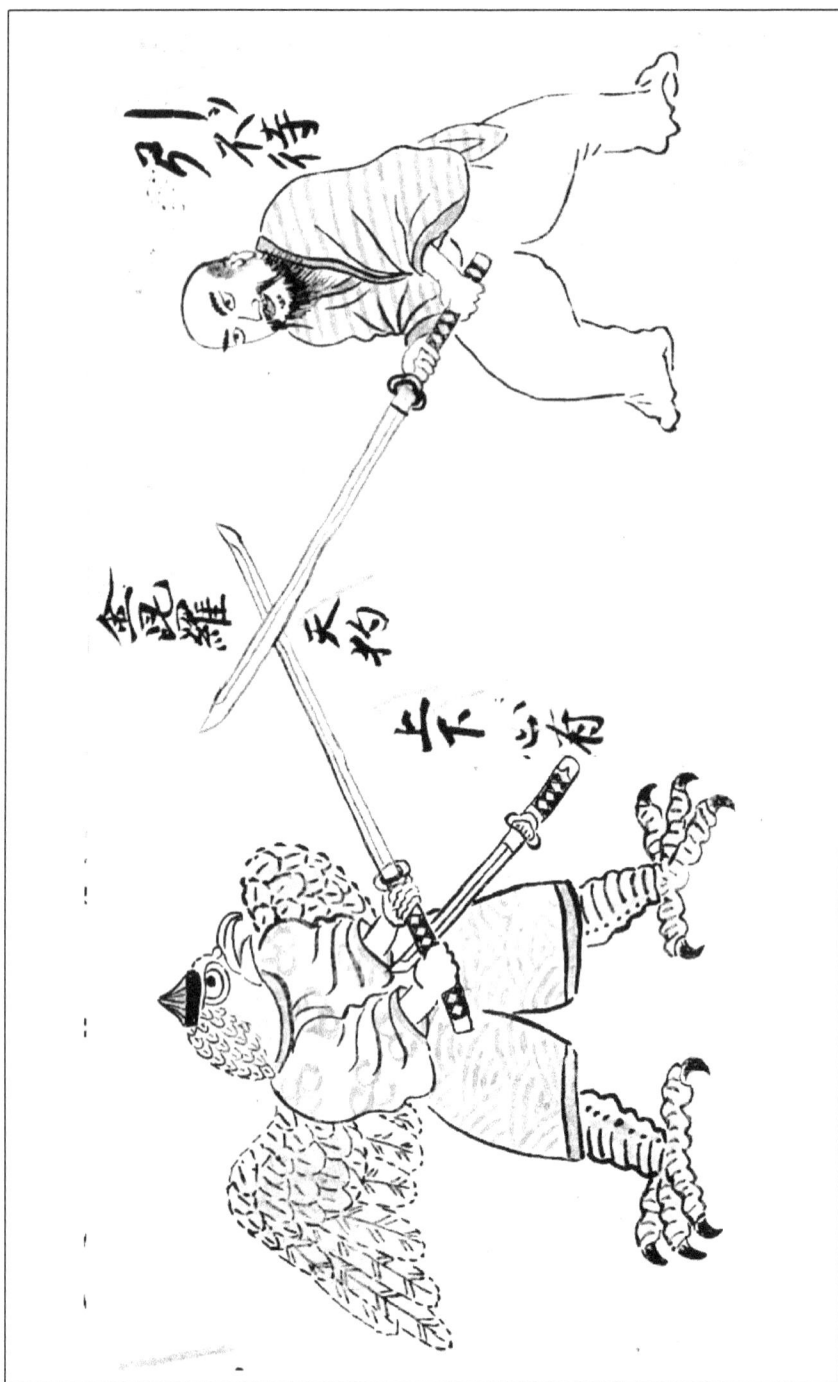

Do not wait for the enemy's attack to draw you in.

金毘羅

天狗

引ヲ不待

Your spirit can go both up and down.

第二 金昆羅天狗 *Dai Ni Konpira Tengu*
引ヲ不待
上下心有

Number Two : Alligator Shaped Buddhist Guardian Deity Tengu
Virtuous Writing by the Light of the Moon
Do not wait for the enemy's attack to draw you in.
Your mind/spirit can go both up and down.

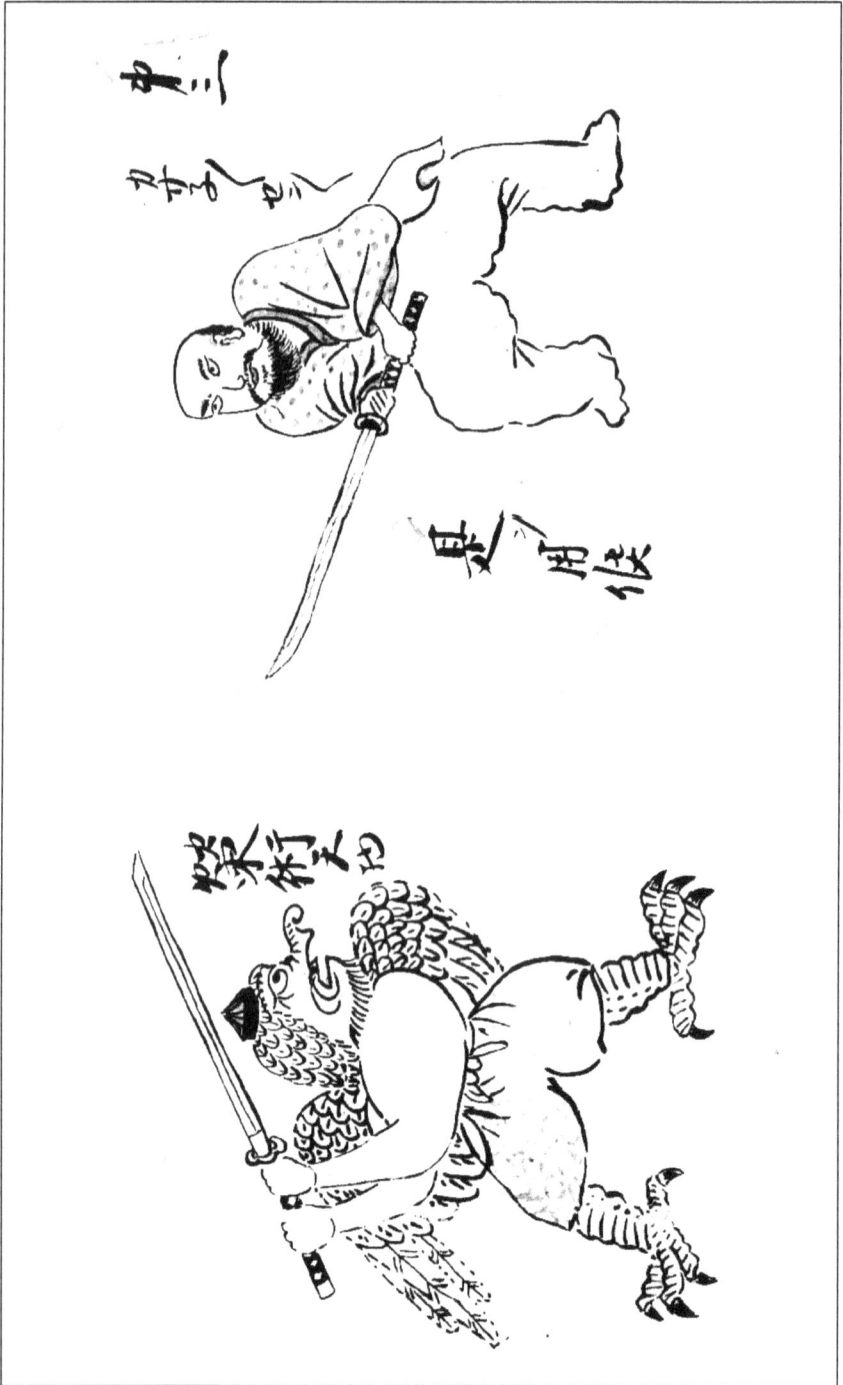

Pile one sword cut upon another, pile one sword cut upon another. Attack before your opponent.

This is the strategy you must use.

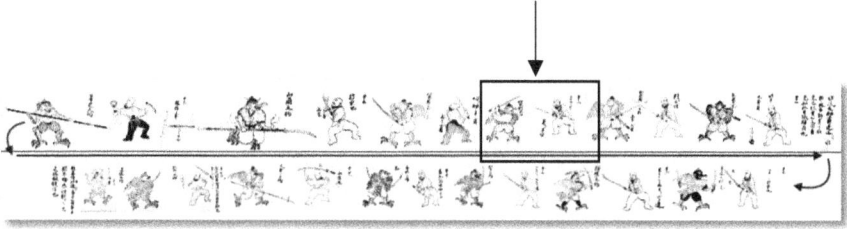

第三 榮術天狗 *Dai San Eijutsu Tengu*
カサネ／＼セン／＼是ヲ用候

Number Three : Overflowing With Technique Tengu
Pile one sword cut upon another, pile one sword cut upon another.
Attack before your opponent. This is the strategy you must use.

一

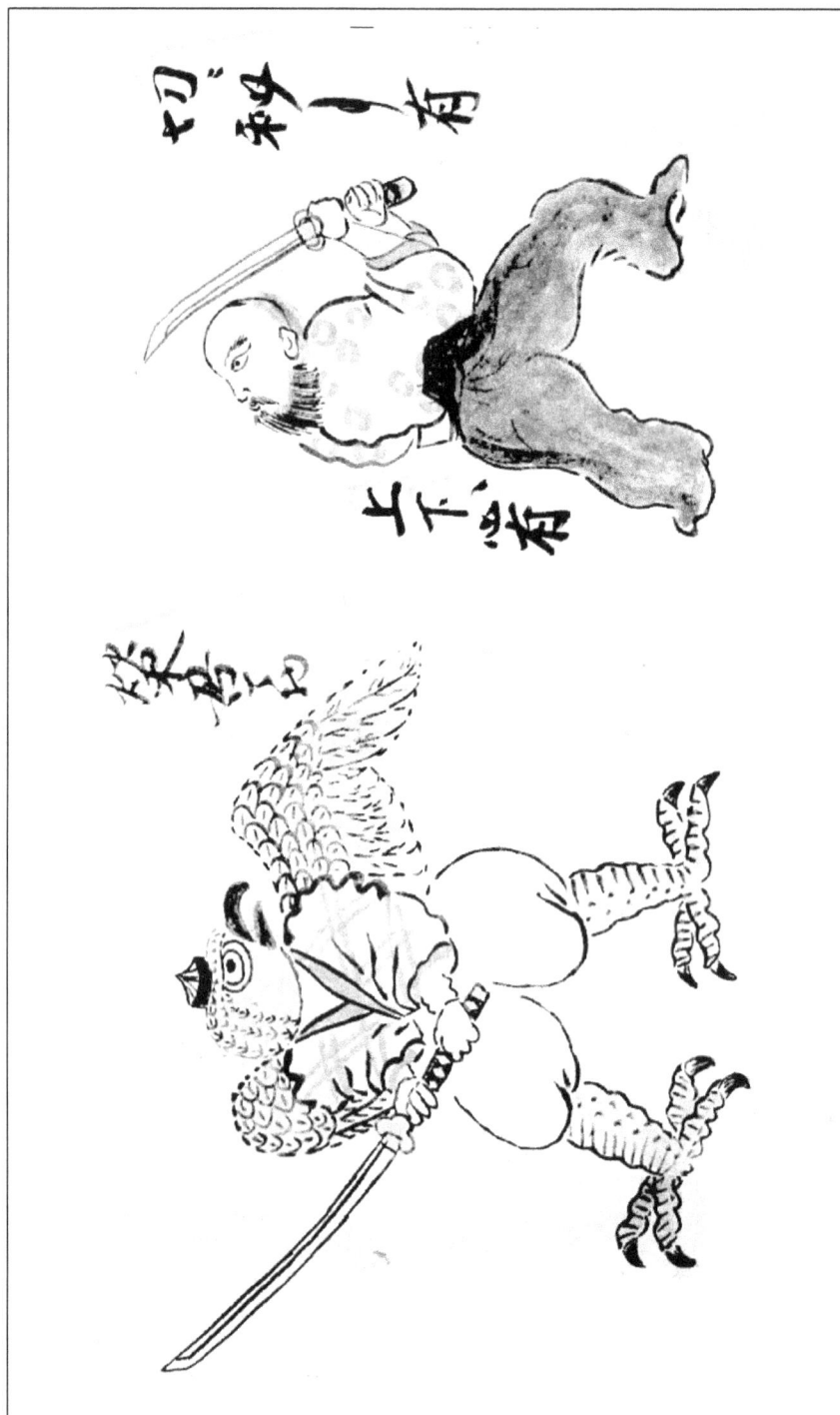

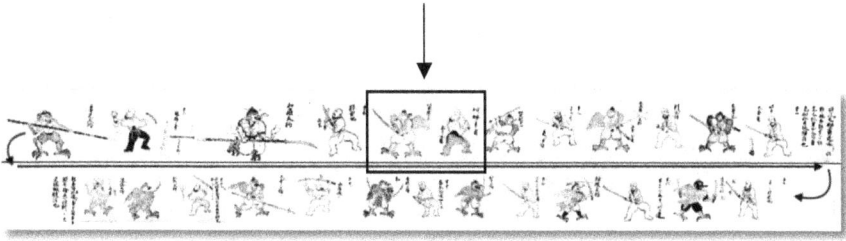

This cut has a secret element.

Your spirit can go both up and down.

第四　榮?天狗　*Dai Yon Ei?*[19] *Tengu*
切二秘事有上下心有

Number Four : Flourishing [?] Tengu
This cut has a secret element. There is a lesson about how to keep your mind above and below.

---

[19] The second Kanji in this Tengu's name is illegible. Possibly 忍 or 居.

73

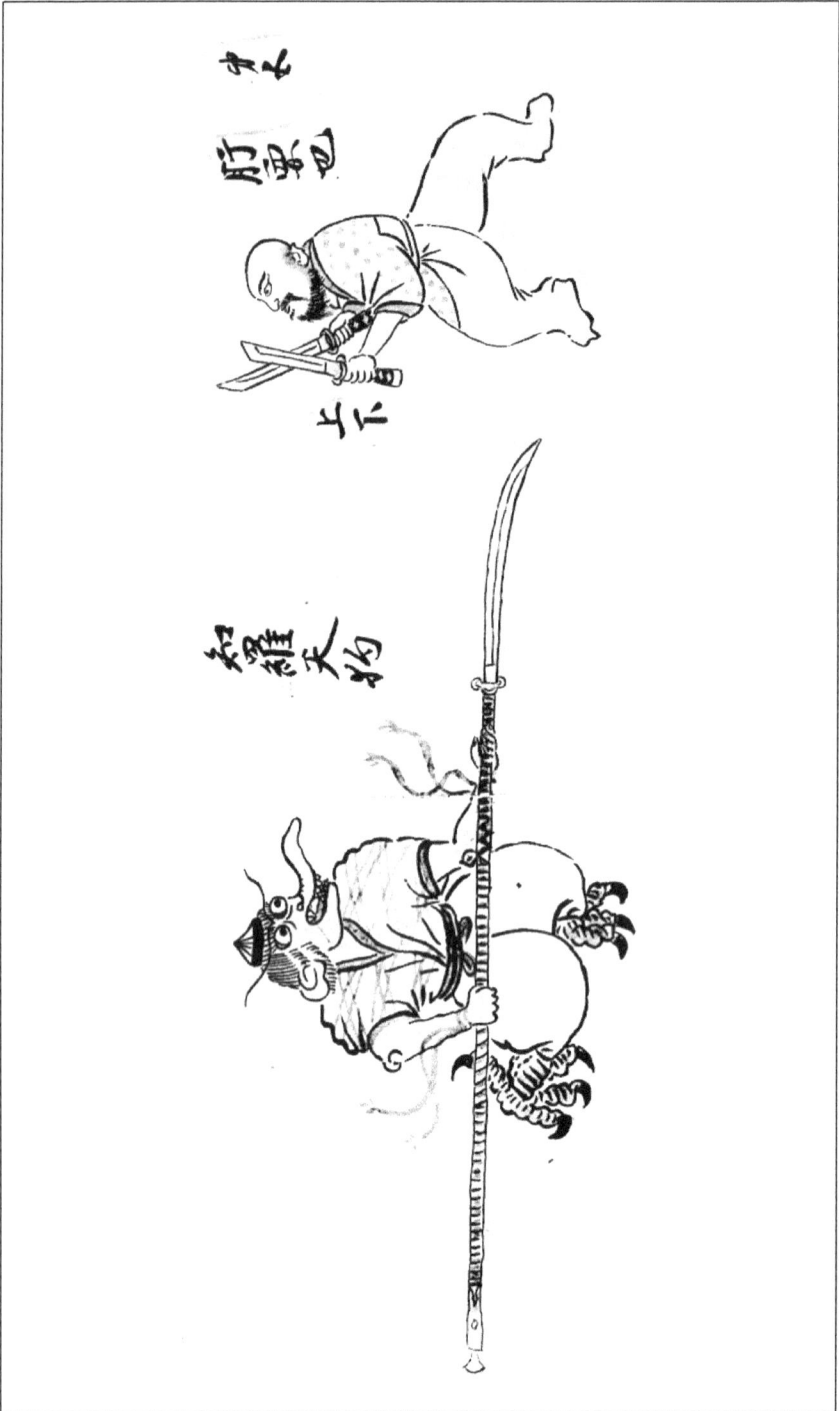

74

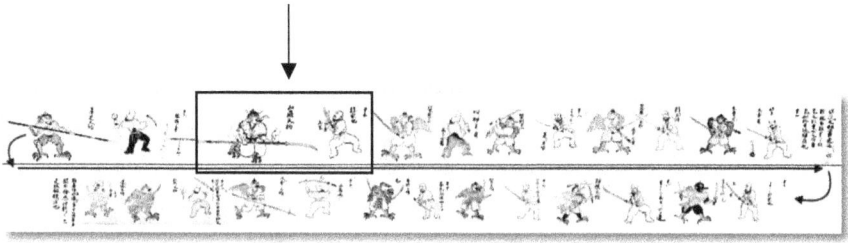

第五
知羅天狗 *Chira Tengu*
肝要也上下

Number Five : Supremely Knowledgeable Tengu
This is a fundamental both above and below.[20]

---

[20] An Edo Era book called *A Lecture on Izuna* 飯縄講式 states that the father of Izuna was the Myozen Tsukiko Tengu 妙善月光 and his mother was the Kinbira Yasha Tengu 金毘羅夜叉. They had 18 princes of which 10 stayed behind to live on the mountain while the rest went out into the world the third of the ten that stayed behind became the Izuna Chira Tengu

第六　尊足天狗　*Dai Roku Sonzoku Tengu*
彼構ノ事　ただ先々ふりたゝさむなく

Number Six : Full of Respect Tengu
This is the stance you should take, however make it seem like your
intent is Sen no Sen, [attacking the moment the attacker decides to
launch a strike.]

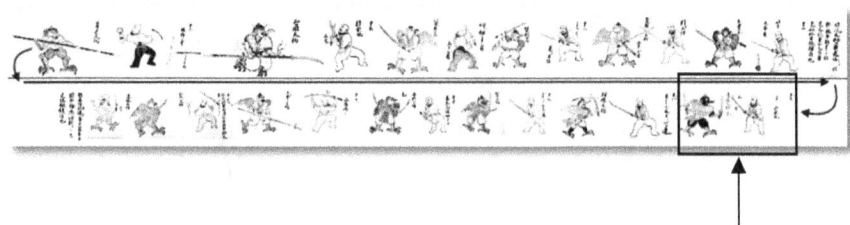

第七 通達天狗 *Dai Nana Tsutatsu Tengu*
光 ヒザソク肝要也上下

Number Seven : One Who Understands the Way Tengu
Quick use of your knees is the fundamental lesson here.
Upper and lower[21].

---

[21] The Kanji Kou 光 is written slightly below the Tengu's name. It's not clear if Kou is part of the Tengu's name or an instruction. The Kanji means brightness, or light emanating.

79

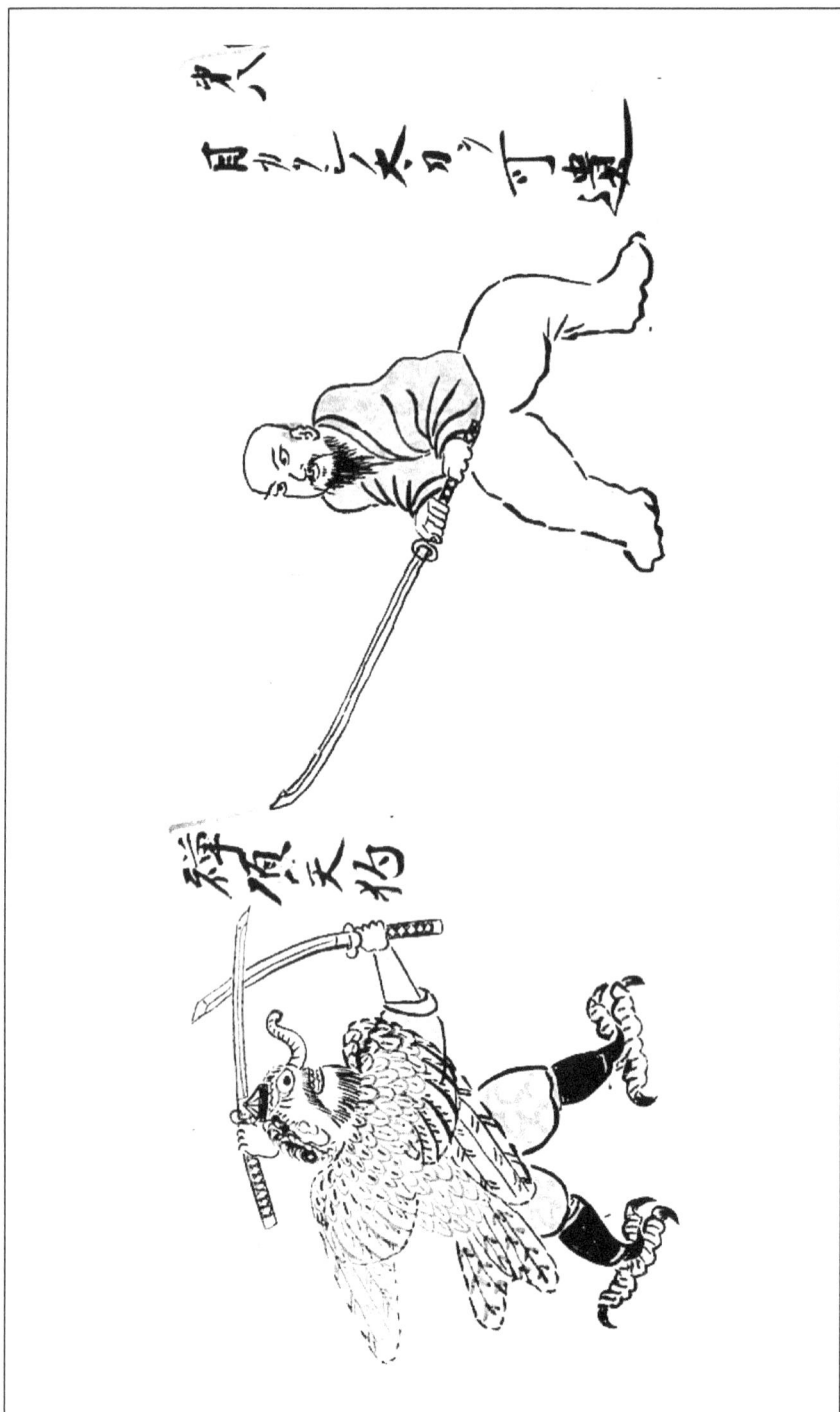

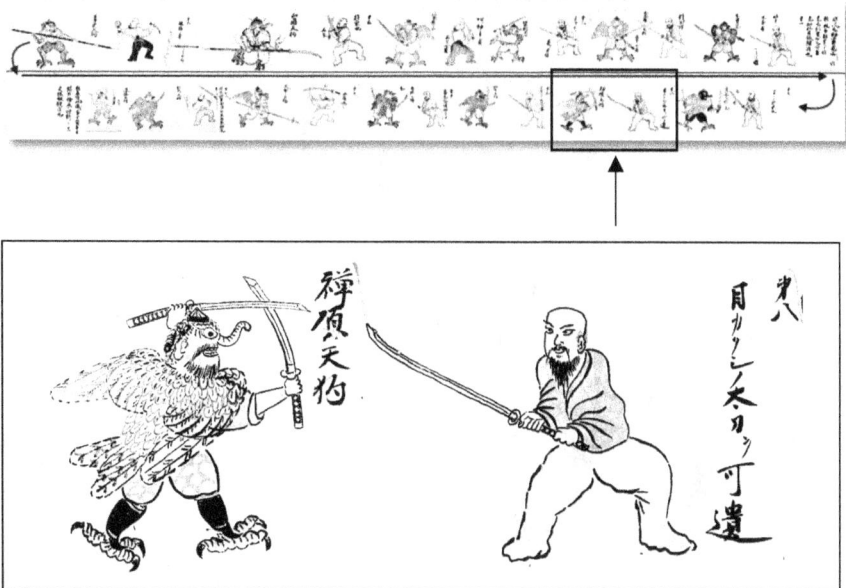

第八 禅頂天狗 *Dai Hachi Zensho Tengu*
目カクシノ太刀ヲ可遣

Number Eight : Peak of Zen Tengu
You should do Mekakushi Tachi, or use your sword as a blindfold.

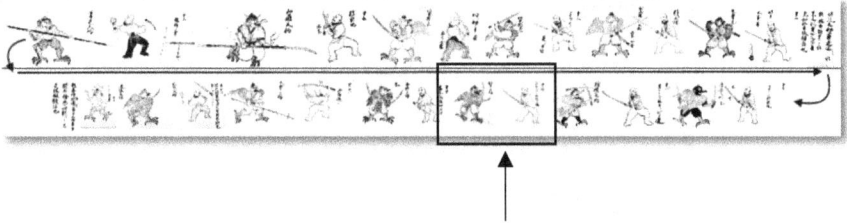

第九 知吉天狗 *Dai Kyu Shiruyoshi Tengu*
小手シハリノ太刀可遣

Number Nine : Auspicious Knowledge Tengu
You should use Kote Shibari no Tachi, Tying the Hands Sword,
method.

Attacks First

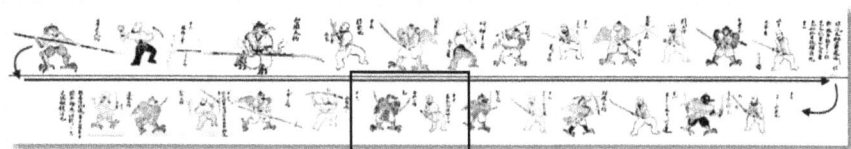

第十　命?天狗 *Dai Ju Mei? Tengu*
先
養老之山渡秘事也

Number Ten : Life [?] Tengu[22]
There is a secret teaching about Mount Yoro here.
Attacks First.

---

[22] The Kanji Saki/Sen 先 is written off to the side, which I have
translated as "attacks first." It means before and could indicate
which sword strikes first. The sword on the right is actually in the
Tengu's left hand. Mount Yoro is in Gifu Prefecture and is also
nicknamed Mount Tengu.

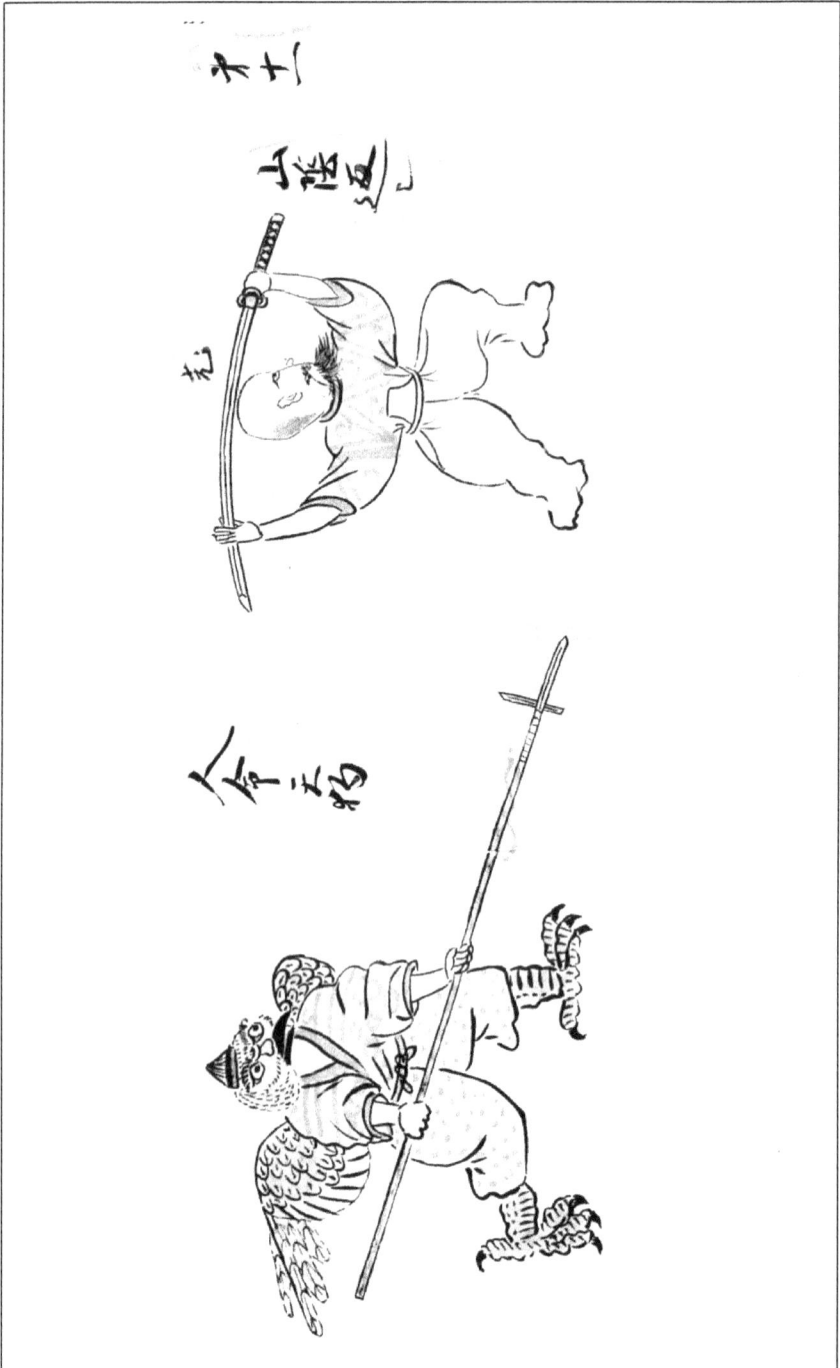

第十一人命天狗 *Dai Juichi Jinmei Tengu*
山陰返シ先

Number Eleven : One Life Tengu
Returning Shadow of the Mountain cut.
Attacks First.

第十二 非頂天狗 *Dai Juni Hicho Tengu*
臨兵闘者皆陣烈在前
怨敵退散ヒツ ツカキフリ

Number Twelve : Never Peak Tengu
Recite *May the presiders over warriors be my vanguard* and with
that it will be as if you have invoked disaster upon the enemy.

Translator's Note :
Kuji

The recitation is the Kuji, Nine Seals, was used by practitioners of Mikkyo esoteric Buddhism, Shugendo, Yamabushi mountain ascetics as well as everyday Japanese people. It originated in a Taoist text from China called *The Book of the Master Who Embraces Simplicity* 抱朴子 in the 4th century AD. It was a prayer to the group of Taoist deities known as the Six Generals 六甲.

The line that was isolated and became the Kuji, or Nine Seals, is in bold. The text in Chinese is below.

抱朴子曰：入名山以甲子開除日以五色繪各五寸懸大石上所求必得又曰入山宜知六甲秘祝祝曰**臨兵鬭者皆陣列前行**。凡九字，常當密祝之，無所不辟。要道不煩，此之謂也。

Translation:
> *To enter a famous mountain, choose an opening day, which can be determined by its cyclical binary. Hang silk of the five colors, each piece five inches wide, from a large rock, so that you may be sure to succeed in your goal. Furthermore, while entering the mountains you must know the Six-Chia secret prayer. It goes like:* ***"May the presiders over warriors be my vanguard!"*** *This nine word prayer must constantly be recited in secret. It means, "May all evils flee me, and the essential procedure present no trouble."*

-Translation from: James R. Ware *Alchemy, Medicine, Religion in the China of A. D. 320: The Nei P'ien of Ko Hung (Pao-p'u Tzu).* Translated [and Edited] by James R. Ware 1966. Page 287

The version in the Aisu Kage School scroll differs from the Chinese original. This is a Buddhist adaptation done probably by Kakuban 覺鑁 (1095–1143) a Shingon Buddhist Priest. Kakubun matched each Kanji to a Bonji Sanskrit character. The reformatted version is based on a mantra of Aminda Nyorai.

Aisu Kage School Scroll :　　　臨兵鬭者皆陣烈在前
Master Who Embraces Simplicity: 臨兵鬭者皆陣列前行

Below is a 19th century version of the Kuji paired with the appropriate hand gestures. This illustration was part of a booklet explaining how to use the Kuji for self-protection from both physical and supernatural dangers as well as bringing good fortune. The details below the pictures indicate the type of seal and which deity is being invoked.

Reading right to left: Rin-Pyo-Toh-Sha-Kai-Jin-Retsu-Zai-Zen This is probably the same reading as the Aisu Kage School Scroll.

ZEN	ZAI	RETSU	JIN	KAI	SHA	TOH	PYO	RIN
前	在	裂	陳	皆	者	闘	兵	臨

On-teki-tai-san 怨敵退散

The four Kanji phrase On-teki-tai-san 怨敵退散 is a kind of curse wishing disaster to befall your enemy or for them to become confused.

道俗天狗

移香傳此道ヲ事十箇年カ
間不捨無由断ヶ工
丈致鍛錬候也
已上

夫致鍛錬候也
間不捨無油断ヶ工
已上移香傳此道ヲ事十箇年カ

道俗天狗 *Dozoku Tengu*

Iko Sensei developed the above techniques after ten years of uninterrupted training. His unwavering dedication enabled him to complete the forging of these methods.[23]

---

[23] The word Kufu 工夫 can mean "devising a clever solution to a problem" as well as "dedicating yourself to spiritual enlightenment." Dozoku is a word that refers to how some people leave the house to pursue the life of a pilgrim or ascetic while others remain at home and live a "normal" life. It is not a critique of either.

摩利支尊天
Marishi-Son-Ten
⇩

同愛洲太郎左衛門尉移香入道
Aisu Taro Saemon no Jo Iko Nyudo
⇩

源久忠
Minamoto Hisatada
⇩

同愛洲右京亮
Aisu Ukyuo no Suke
⇩

源朝信
Minamoto Asanobu
⇩

Note: In scroll 1 Shinzan Hikoshiro 新山彦四郎 is recorded as next in line but is not in this scroll.
⇩

同湯原次郎兵衛尉藤原雅景
Yuhara Jiro Hyoe no Jo Fujiwara Masakage
Note: Hyoe no Jo is an official position in a Domain. Scroll two adds "Fujiwara Masakage" to Yuhara's name.

花押
Kao

宇喜多助四郎殿相傳
Transmitted to Lord Ukita Sukesuke Shiro

天正四年三月吉日
On an auspicious day in March of the 4th year of Tensei 1576

Translator's Note:

Tengu

This merging of Shinto Kami and Buddhist deities began in the 6th century when Buddhism was introduced from China. The Japanese never relinquished their native Shinto beliefs and the two religions existed side by side, and began merging to a degree. This is called *Shinbutsu-shūgō* 神仏習合.

Eijutsu Tengu another name for Atago Gongen, a Buddhist deity, Bodhisattva Jizo that has merged with a native Japanese god or Kami. Shugendo practitioners began the practice on Mount Atago in Kyoto, however there are hundreds of Mount Atago all over Japan with Shrines to Atago Gogon. Practitioners of Sangaku Shinko, reverence of mountains also worship Atago Mountains. This deity protects against fire.

History of Atago Mountain 愛宕山

The Shrine on Atago mountain was founded by En no Ozune 役小角, also known as En no Gyoja along with Taicho 泰澄 around 701-704 AD. They enshrined Buddhist deities 地蔵五仏 and the great Tengu god Gongen 天狗大魔王の示現. 戸隠山とともに飯綱山

The God of War 軍神信仰

The Shogun Jizo is also enshrined at Atago Mountain. The shrine on top of the mountain was also known as Haku-unji, White Cloud Temple, a Buddhist temple. During the Sengoku Era Samurai prayed to the Atago Gengon since he was considered to be the God of War. He was a manifestation of the Victorious Army Jizo 勝軍地蔵.

Overview of the deities at Mount Atago

地蔵菩薩 Jizo Bosatsu	愛宕太郎坊天狗 榮術天狗 Atago Tarobo also known as Eijutsu Tengu

毘沙門天 Bishamonten (One of the Four Guardians of Buddhism)	勝軍地蔵 将軍地蔵 Shogun Jizo God of War	不動明王 Fudo Myo-o Immovable Lord of Light

役行者と前鬼後鬼

En no Gyoja (the founder of Atago) along with Zenki and Goki (a married demon couple that assist him.)

The oldest document about Izuna Kongen is a Muromachi Era document called The Origins of Kenkoji Temple on Mount Togakushi 戸隠山顕光寺流記. Within the book there is a line about Tengu,

吾は是れ、日本第三の天狗なり。願わくは此の山の傍らに侍し、権現の慈風に当たりて三熱の苦を脱するを得ん

I, [Izuna Kongen], am the third Tengu of Japan. If you seek my blessing wait by the side of this mountain. You will feel the benevolent breeze of the [Nine headed dragon] Kongen and the three fiery sufferings will befall you. [You will be burned by heat: hot wind will sear your skin and hot sand will fry your flesh and bones down to the marrow. You will be assaulted by poisoned wind which will blow your clothes and jewelry away. Finally, the Konjicho bird will feed you to its young.]

The previous Enpi Mokuroku, Leaping Monkey Scroll contains the line, "There is a separate scroll for middle-level students." That line could be referring to The Tengu Scroll.

Professors Miyamoto Koki and Uozumi Takashi wrote in International Budo University Journal,

The pairing of Tengu in these documents is indicative of pre-Edo Era marital arts documents. Post 1600, most illustrated sword documents showed both combatants as human. Since Tengu live in the mountains, they seem to indicate a connection to Shugendo and Yamabushi ascetic training along with Sangaku Shinko, worshiping of mountains. The long noses are indicative of transcendental power. The use of Kuji also adds Mikkyo, esoteric Buddhist elements.

-愛洲陰之流目録の調査報告 2012
A Research Report on the Four Scrolls of Aisu Kage School

AISU IKOSAI・愛洲言移香

Scroll 3
仕相之太刀

•

Shiai no Tachi
The Dueling Sword Scroll
1576

仕相之太刀 *Shiai no Tachi* Dueling Sword
一のべたち Extension Sword

一はねたち Hane Tachi

Deflecting Sword

一ちのたち *Chi no Tachi*
Grounded Sword
Blood Sword[24]

Translator's Note:

---

[24] Since "Chi" is written in the Hiragana alphabet it is impossible to determine the meaning of this stance or technique. I have given two possible interpretations.

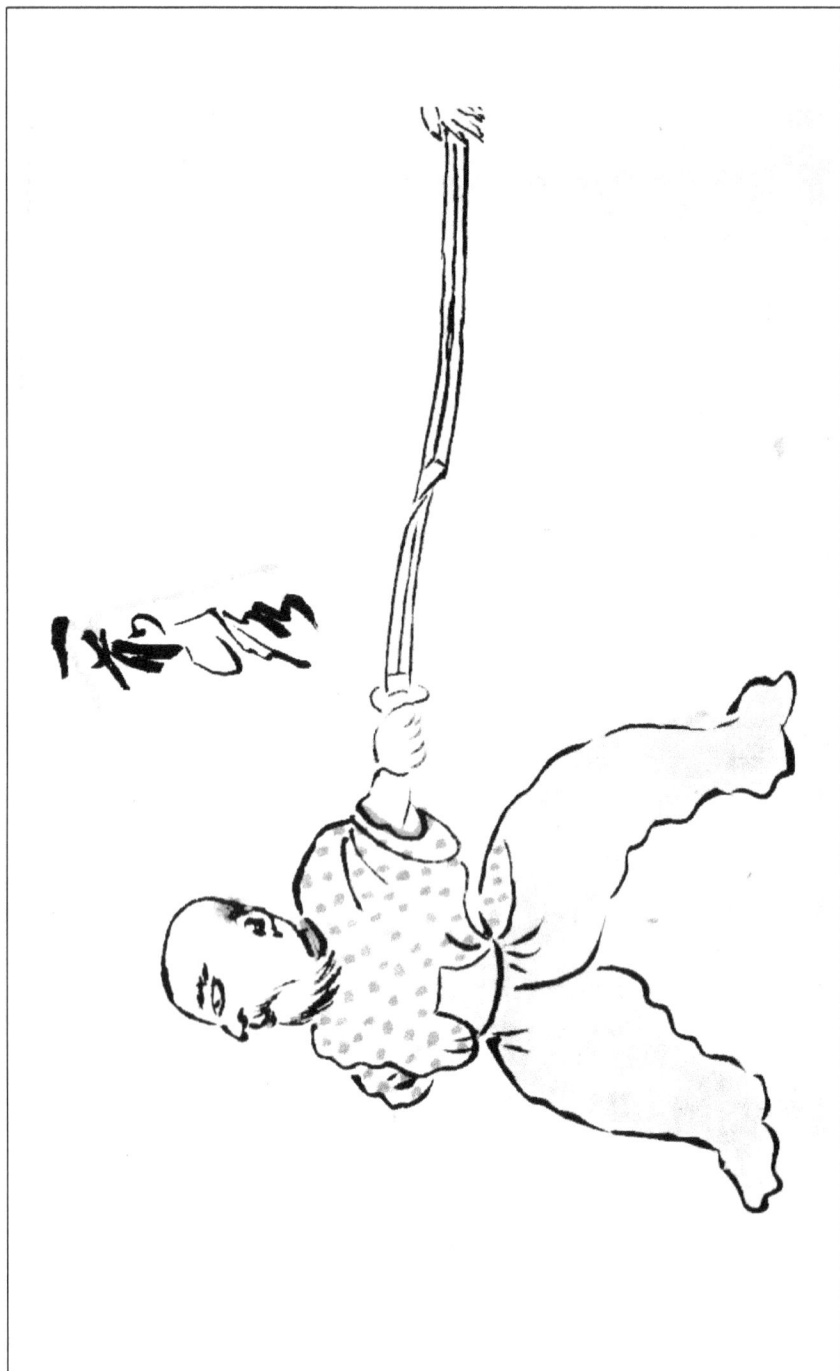

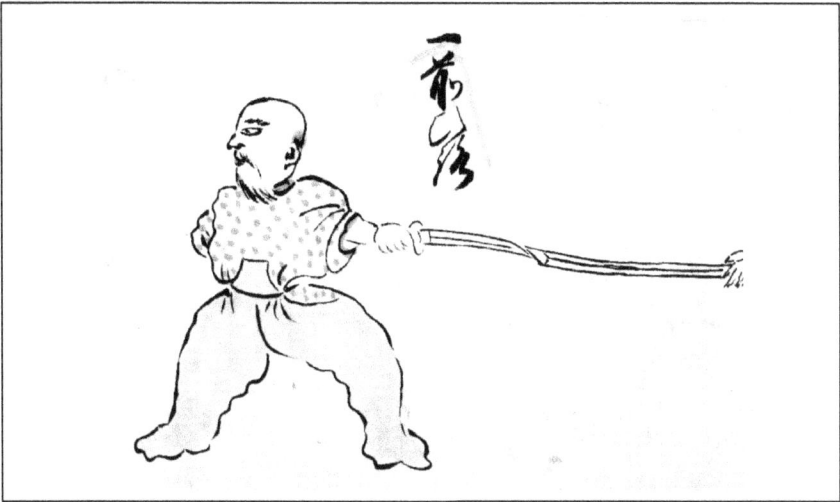

一前ひろ *Maehiro*
Wide Open Front[25]

---

[25] The swords of these two illustrations are touching but it is not clear if the two techniques are connected.

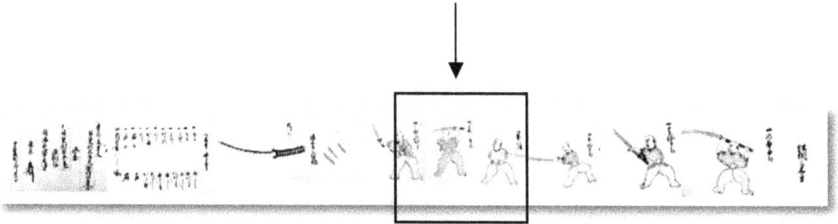

一はつしきり *Hatsu Shikiri*
First Separation

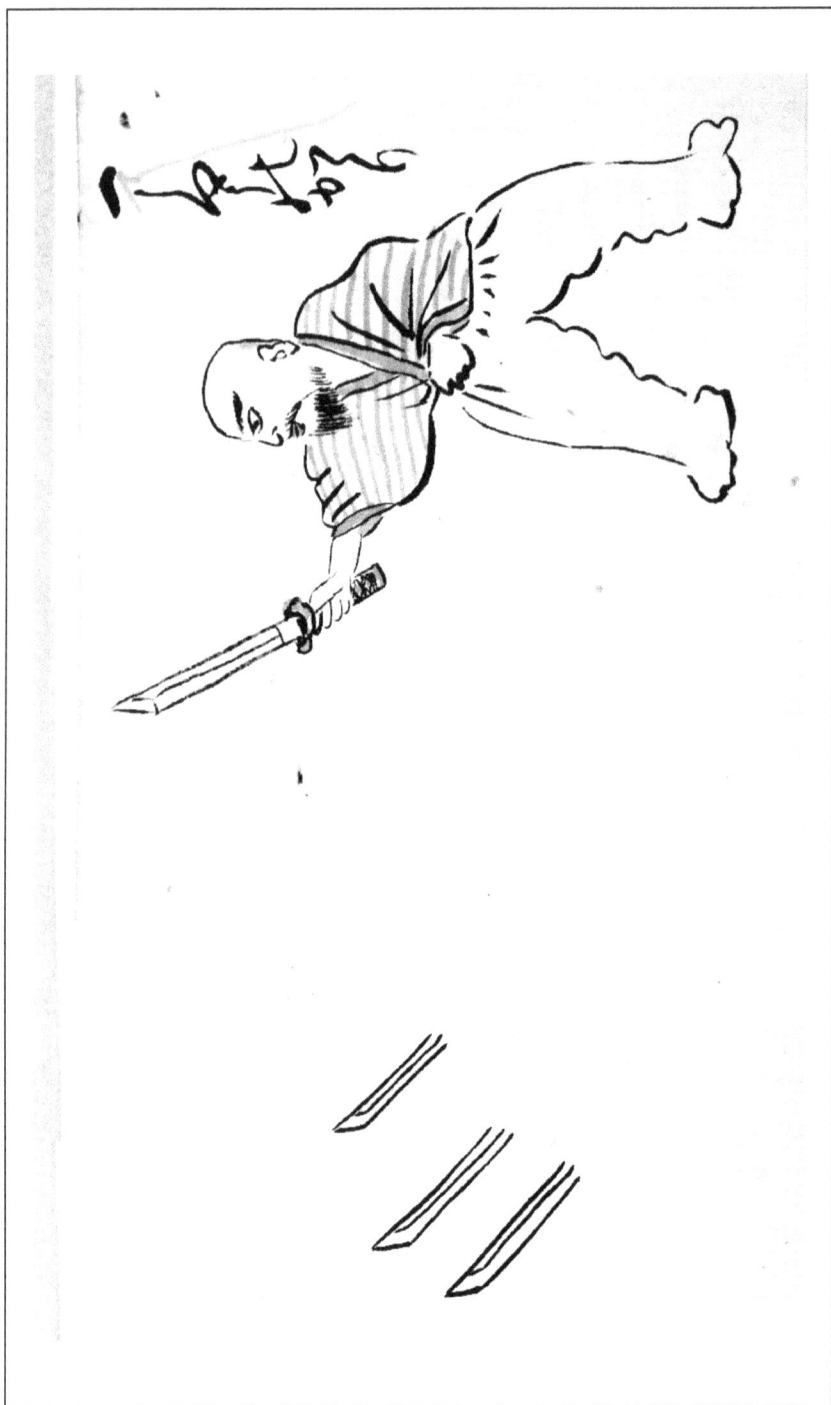

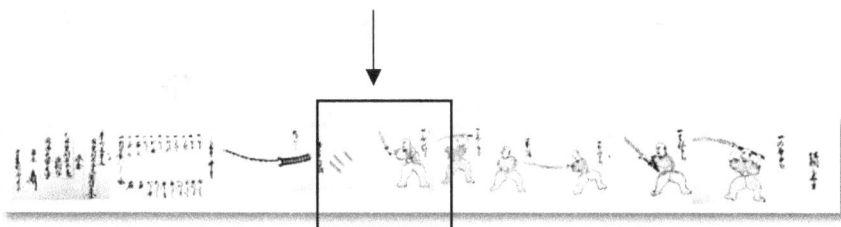

一しやうのかかり *Sho no Kakari*

First Attack

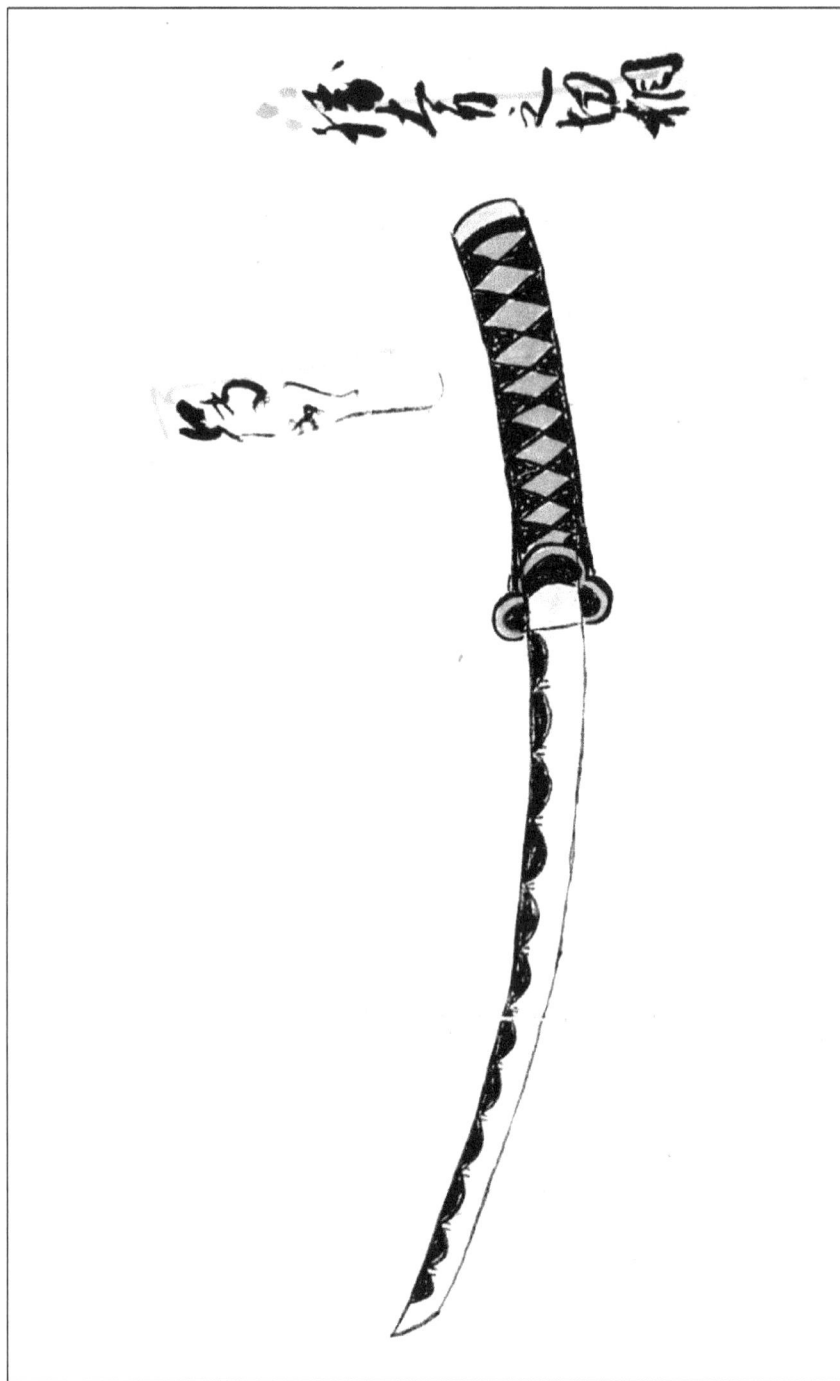

勝太刀之切相 *Katsu Tachi no Kiriai*
口傳おゝし *Kuden Ooshi*

How to win a duel with your Tachi
There are many oral transmissions.

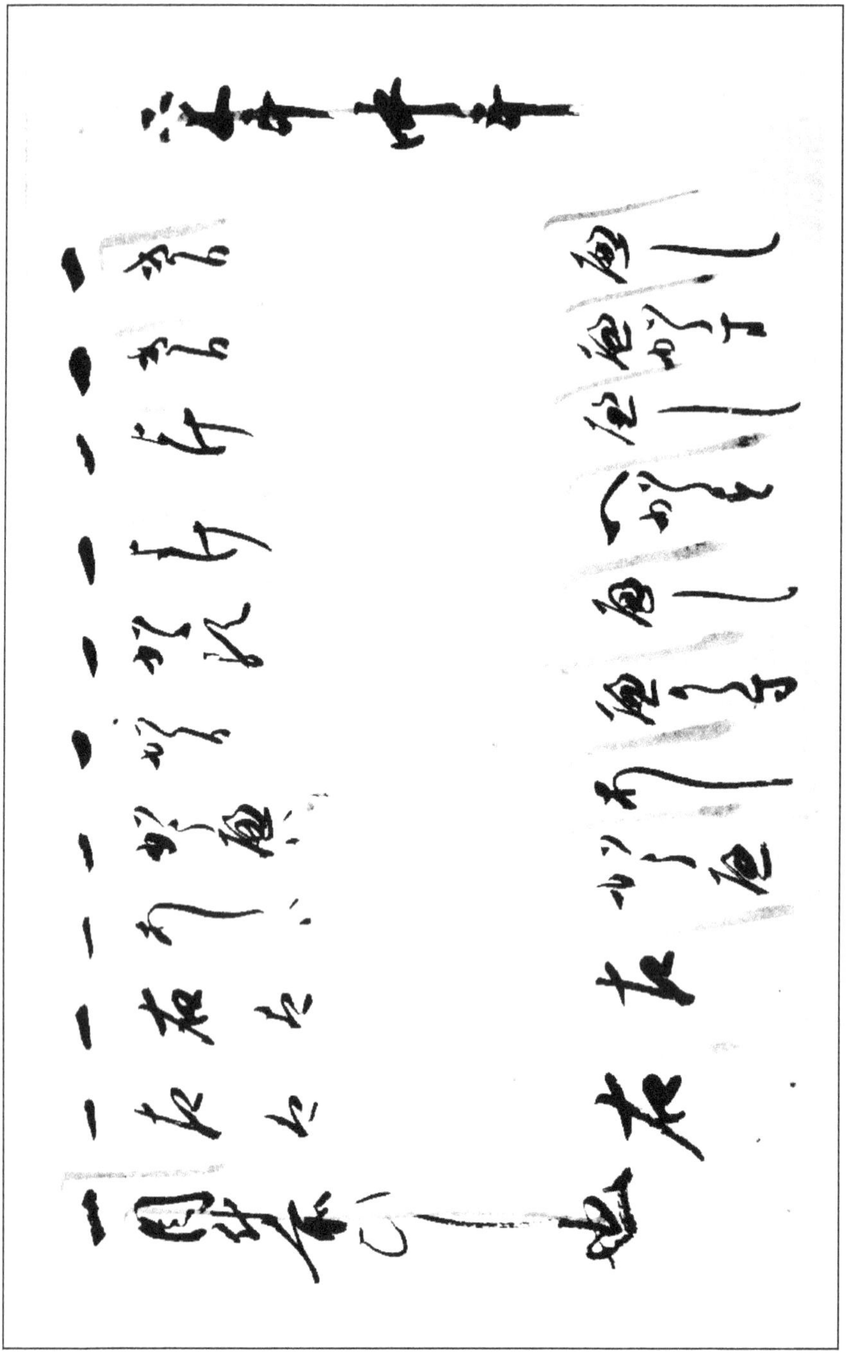

一きる　　べし
一きる　　べからず
一よけ　　べし
一かゝる　べからず
一かゝる　べし
一かゝらへハ　べからず
一あしはかゝらへ　あし
一右は　　　左
一左は　　　右
一目付所ひし也以上

上手 *Uwate* Upper Hand 中手 *Nakate* Middle Hand

Cut → You should
Cut → You should not .
Avoid → You should
Avoid → You should not
Take the Initiative → You should
Take the Initiative → You should not
If the attacker takes the Initiative → Legs and Feet

If the attacker's legs and feet take the Initiative:
In case of Right → Left
In case of Left → Right

You should be conscious of where you place your eyes.
End

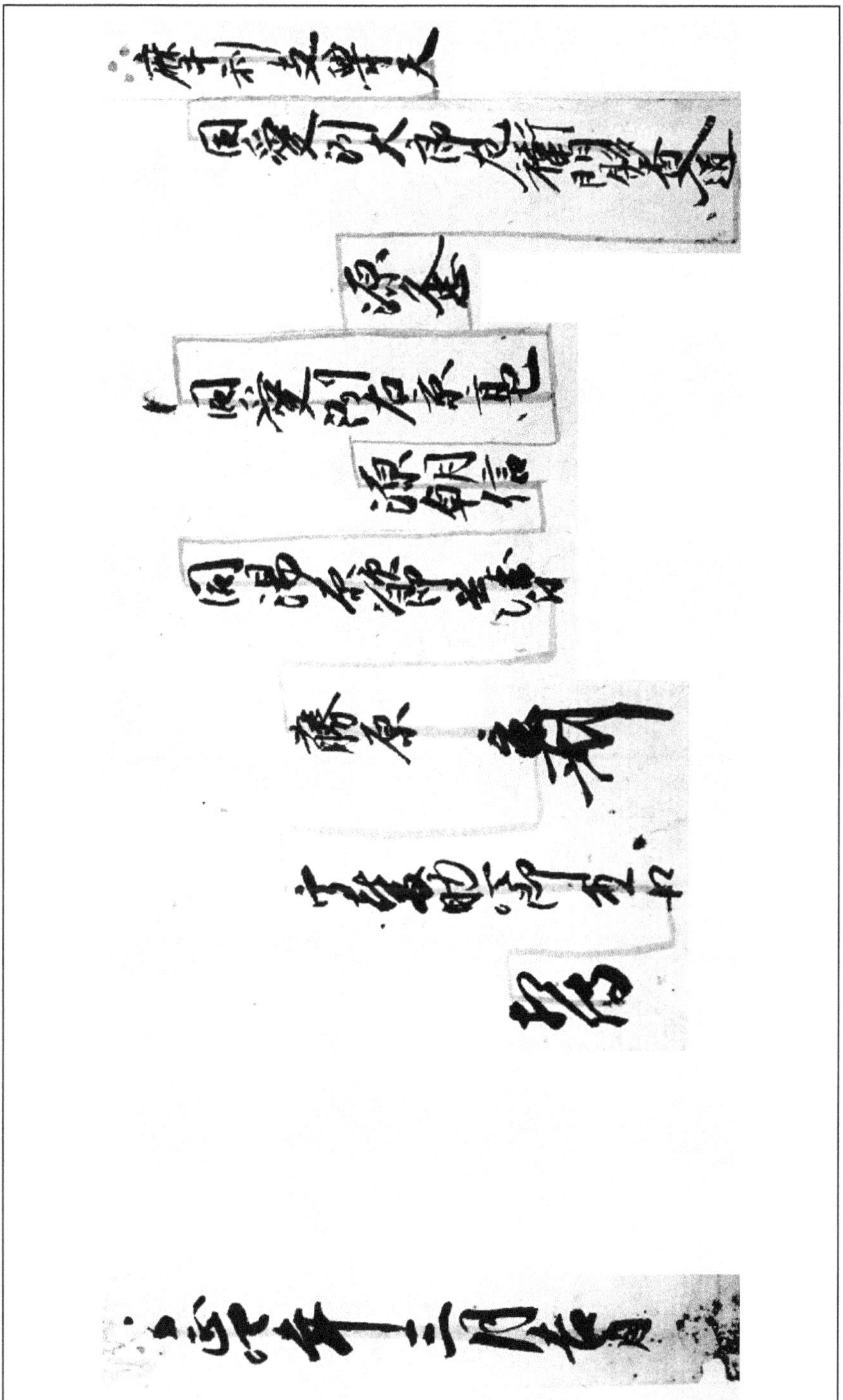

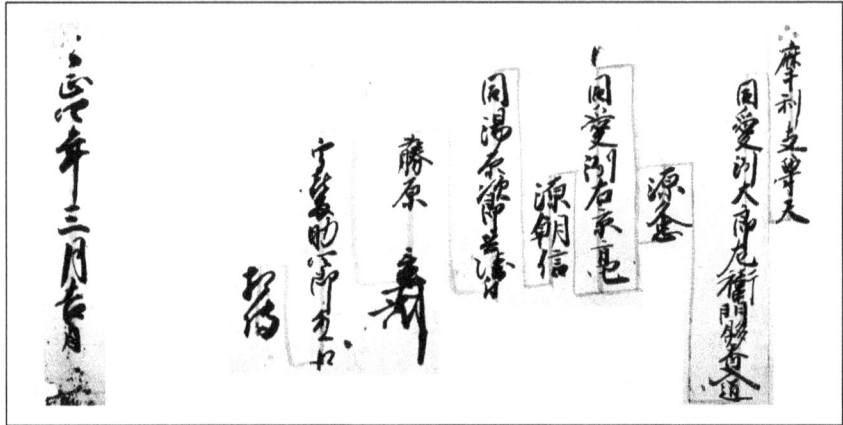

摩利支尊天
Marishi-Son-Ten
⇩

同愛洲太郎左衛門尉移香入道
Aisu Taro Saemon no Jo Iko Nyudo
⇩

源久忠
Minamoto Hisatada
⇩

同愛洲右京亮
Aisu Ukyuo no Suke
⇩

源朝信
Minamoto Asanobu
⇩

Note: In scroll 1 Shinzan Hikoshiro 新山彦四郎 is recorded as next in line but is not in this scroll.
⇩

同湯原次郎兵衛尉藤原雅景
Yuhara Jiro Hyoe no Jo Fujiwara Masakage
Note: Hyoe no Jo is an official position in a Domain. Scroll two adds "Fujiwara Masakage" to Yuhara's name.

花押
Kao

宇喜多助四郎殿江
Transmitted to Lord Ukita Sukesuke Shiro

天正四年三月吉日
On an auspicious day in March of the 4th year of Tensei 1576

Scroll 4
目かくし

•

Mekakushi
Blindfolded
1576

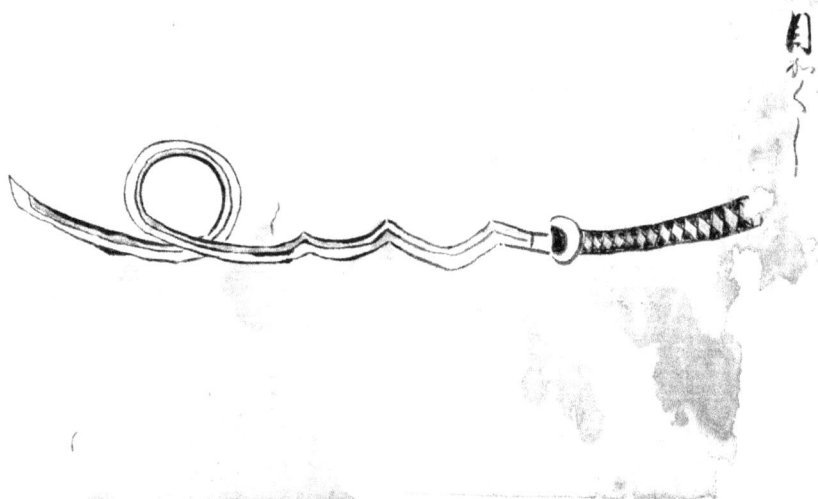

Scroll 4
目かくし *Mekakushi*
Blindfold

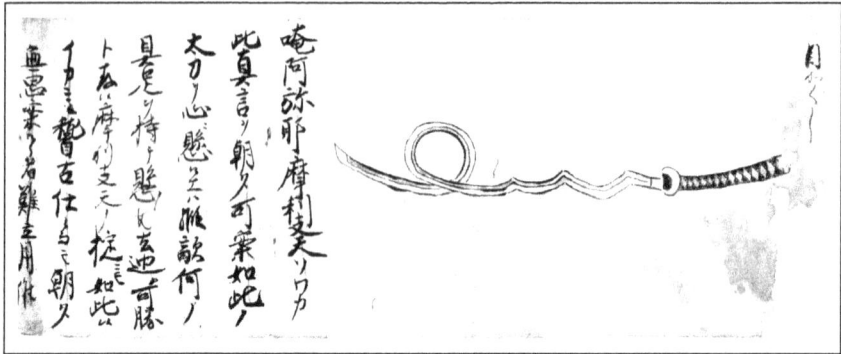

This is called the Blindfold Scroll. Mekakushi, or blindfold, can mean something physically blocking the eyes or a partition that is placed just inside the entrance to a house. It serves to block the visitors' line of sight so they can't see within your house.[26]

---

[26] The scroll is cut off and the Okugaki, or postscript, which contains the lineage of the school and a date are missing. However according to Professors Uozumi and Miyamaoto,

Based on the type of paper, shape, calligraphy style and ink it was composed at the same time and by the same person as the other three scrolls.

-愛洲陰之流目録の調査報告 2012
A Research Report on the Four Scrolls of Aisu Kage School

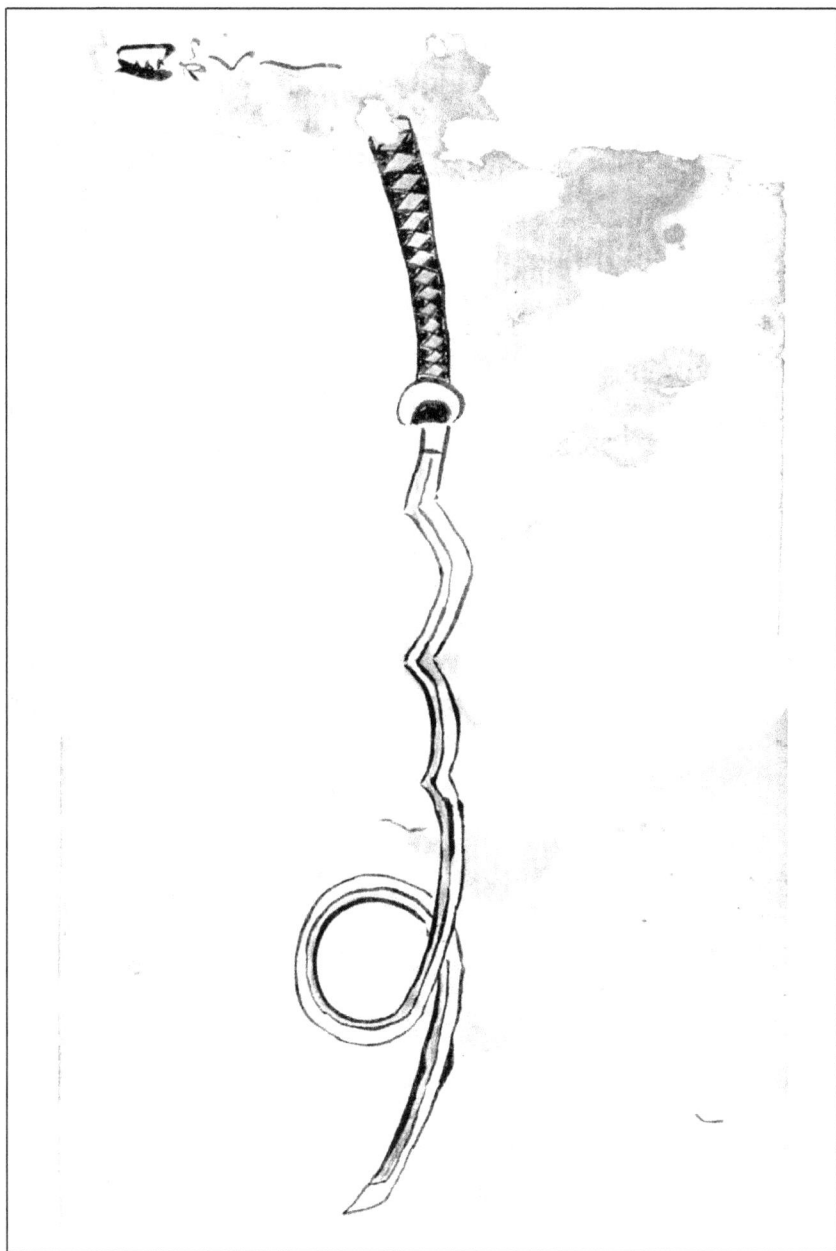

目かくし
Mekakushi
Blindfold

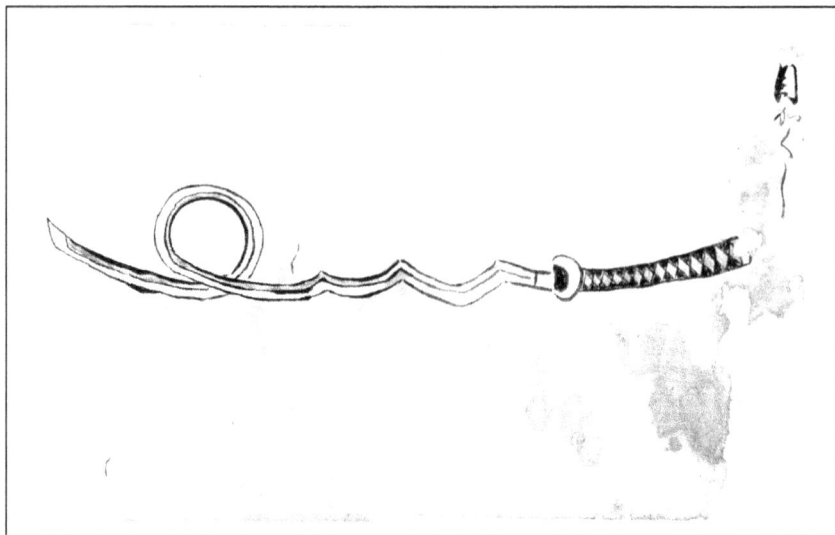

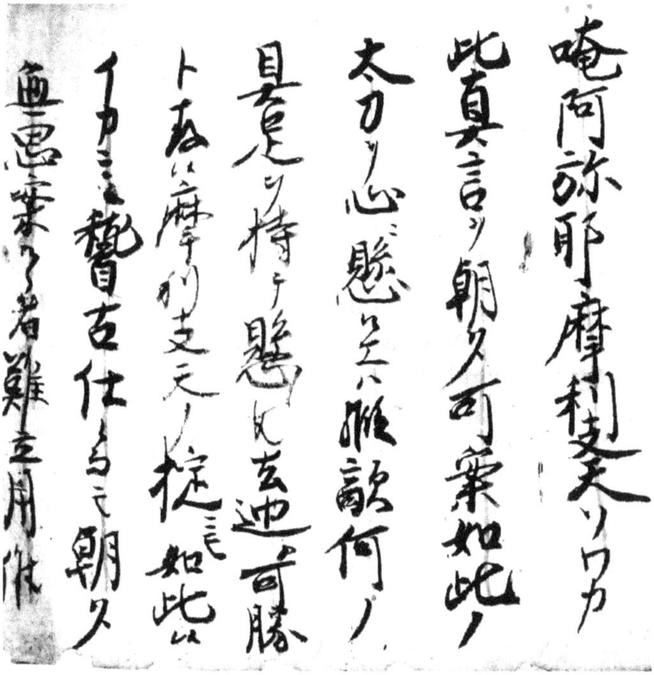

唵阿弥　耶摩利支天ソワカ

此真言ヲ朝夕可案如此ノ

太刀ヲ心ニ懸候エハ縦　敵何ノ

具足ヲ持テ懸ル去　迊可勝

ト在以摩利支天ノ掟ニモ如此以

イカニモ稽古仕候而モ朝夕

無思案候て者難立用候

This mantra should be repeated every morning and night:

On-ah-bi Marishiten Sowaka
Praise Marishiten and may I remain in his grace.

You should ingrain this way of the sword into your body. If you do, no matter what weapon your enemy holds you will be able to sweep it away and emerge victorious. However these methods, which have been handed down to us by Marishiten require the learner to not only train morning and night but consider the lessons that have been taught. Failing to do so will mean the student will not learn.

Four Scrolls of The Shadow Sword School
End

新陰之流猿飛の目録

•

Shin Kage no Ryu Enpi no Mokuroku
New Shadow School Leaping Monkey
Catalogue of Techniques
1605

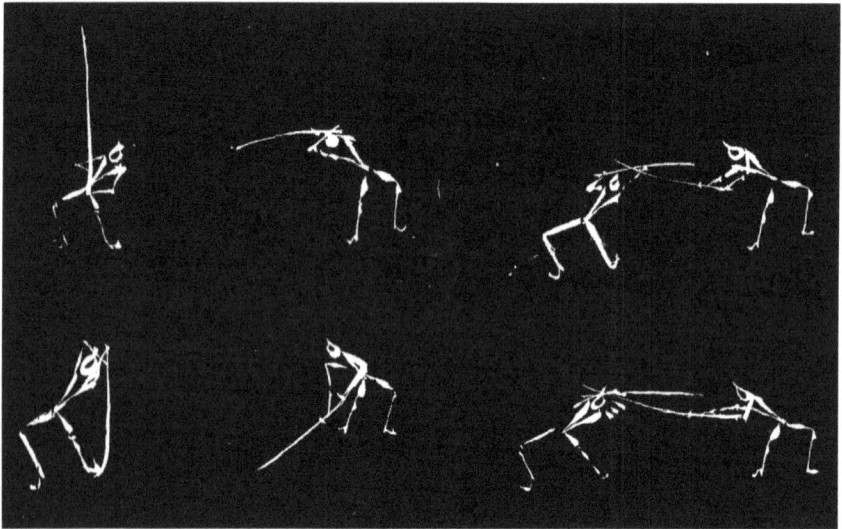

Translator's Introduction:

新陰疋田流
Shinkage Hikita School

Hikita Bungorō Kagetada 疋田文五郎景兼 (1537~1605) was a high-level student or possibly the nephew of Kamiizumi Hidetsuna. His school was known as Hikita Ryu written either as 疋田流 or 匹田流 and consisted of Kenjutsu, Sojutsu (spear fighting) as well as other martial arts.

Overview of this scroll:
New Shadow School Leaping Monkey Record of Techniques
Issued 1605

Yamakage	Enkai	Enpi	Introduction

Lineage	Uranami	Ukibune	Gekkage

新陰之流猿飛の目録

およそ猿飛は懸待表裏の行。五箇の旨趣を以て肝要となす。所謂五箇は眼・意・身・手・足なり。この位能々鍛錬に於いて浅きより深きに至る秘術これあるべきものなり。

The purpose of, Enpi, or Leaping Monkey, is to use Sen no Sen (attacking first) or Go no Sen (waiting for the enemy to attack first) as well as making your opponent thinking you are doing one or the other. Making use of the Five Points is fundamental to this. The Five points are : Sight, Spirit, Body, Hands, Feet. You must train relentlessly in these stances in order to move from a shallow to a deep understanding of these secret techniques.

猿飛 Enpi Leaping Monkey

猿廻 Enaki Circling Monkey

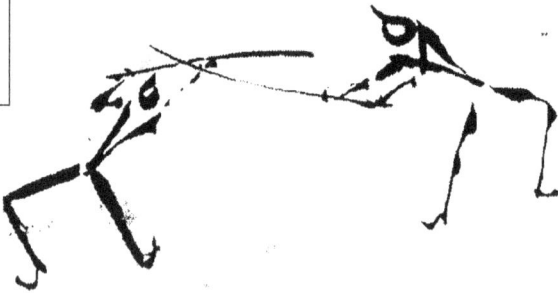

山陰 Yamakage Shadow of the Mountain

月影 Gekkage Moon and Shadow

浮舟 Ukibune Float Like a Boat

浦波 Uranami Reversing Wave

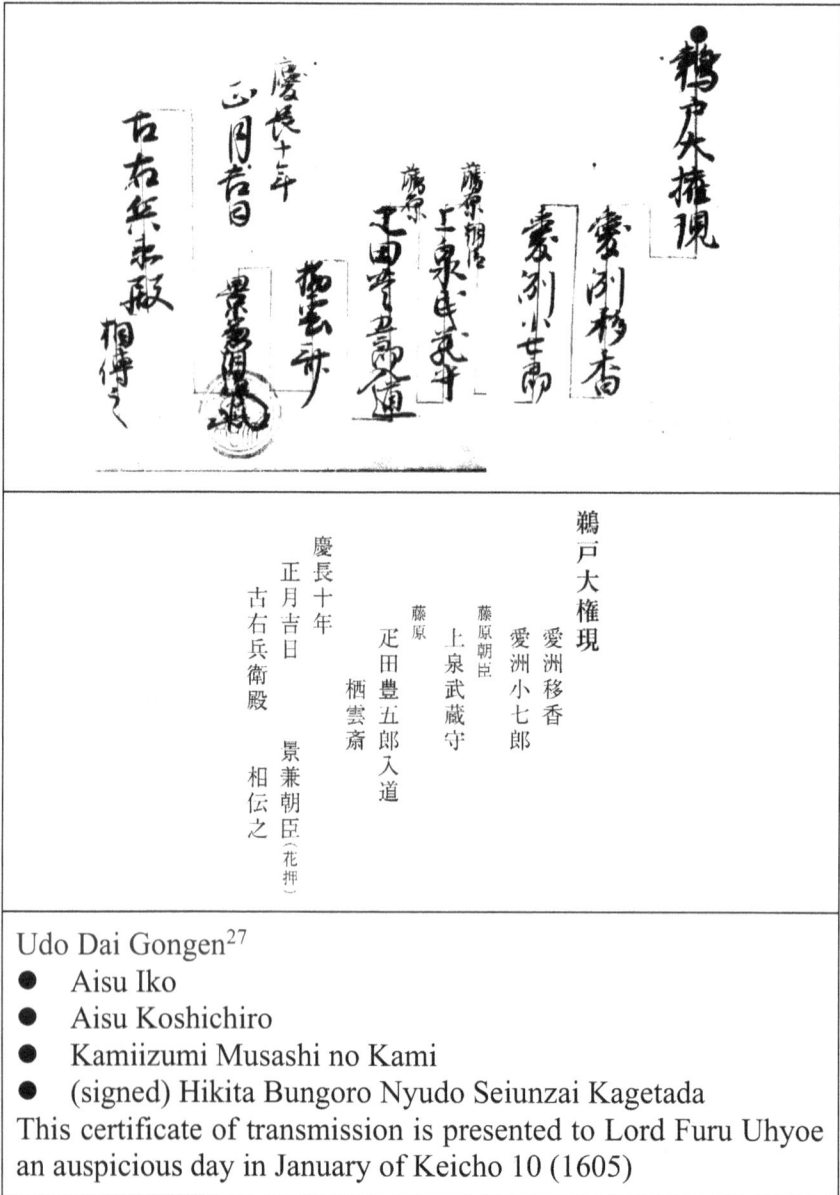

鵜戸大権現

愛洲移香
愛洲小七郎
藤原朝臣
上泉武蔵守
藤原
疋田豊五郎入道
栖雲斎

慶長十年
正月吉日
古右兵衛殿
景兼朝臣（花押）
相伝之

Udo Dai Gongen[27]
- Aisu Iko
- Aisu Koshichiro
- Kamiizumi Musashi no Kami
- (signed) Hikita Bungoro Nyudo Seiunzai Kagetada

This certificate of transmission is presented to Lord Furu Uhyoe an auspicious day in January of Keicho 10 (1605)

[27] This is the name of the deity enshrined at what is now Udo Shrine in Kyushu. Udo is derived from words meaning "empty" and "cave" referring to the chamber where Aisu meditated. The ceremonies at this temple also focus on the cormorant so the name is "Door of the Cormorant."

136

新陰流天狗巻
Shinkage Ryu Tengu
New Shadow School Mountain Goblin Scroll

▪

1605

新陰流天狗書巻

抑天狗者生不滅有

躰不見有名不答

在住所無家如或

辻風或木魂㕥此術

尤、尔也縣不為縣待

不為待表不為裏

故裏又不為裏

上下天下而決勝負

不思議神変也

依之天狗書云々

140

New Shadow School Mountain Goblin Scroll

Most people know that Tengu, mountain goblins, are immortal creatures who have bodies without form.   If you ask their name, they won't respond. Though they dwell in places, they have no home. If they do appear, it is only as a whirlwind or as the soul of a tree. This is how the power of the Tengu works.

Attacks never turn out to be attacks. Defenses never turn out to be defenses. The technique a Tengu shows turns out not be the one shown.   Therefore, his hidden intent turns out not to be his hidden intent. The Tengu fights from both above and below, as if both were the heavens. A mysterious and divine technique. This is what is taught to us in the *Scroll of the Mountain Goblin*.

Korin-bo : Tall Grove Tengu

高林房

Fugen-bo : Seeing the Wind Tengu

風眼房

Taro-bo : Young Man Tengu

Ei-i-bo : Show-off Tengu

Chiranbo : Complete Knowledge Under Heaven

Karanbo : Raging Fire Tengu

Shutokubo : Versed In Morality Tengu

Konpirabo : Mythical Water Dragon (That guards the Buddha)

(no text)

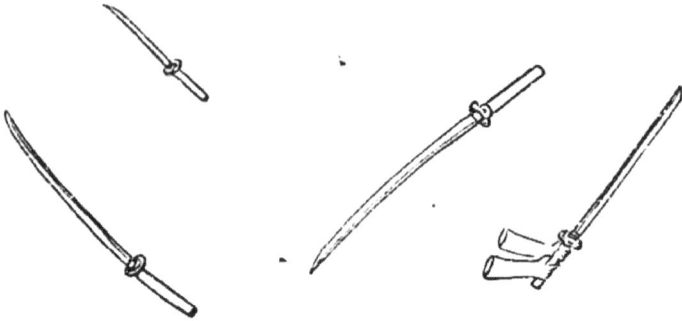

上泉伊勢守

藤原信綱

西一頃
須高兼

山本三宄
藤原某

豊か郡廿年
七月吉日

Kamiizumi Ise no Kami Fujiwara Nobutsuna
[unknown]
Yamamoto [unknown]
An auspicious day in July 1605

柳生剣法許状

Yagu Kenpo Kyojo
Certification in Yagyu Sword Art

·

A New Translation of *The Tengu Scroll*
From :
Yagyu Shin Kage Ryu
Yagyu New Shadow School of Sword
Original Scroll from 1601
Text added in 1707

Translator's Note:

Certification in Yagyu Sword Art

Kamiizumi the Guardian of Ise developed Shin Kage Ryu, The New Shadow School, from his understanding of the Aisu Shadow School. In 1565 Kamiizumi passed on the headmastership to Yagyu Sekishusai Munetoshi, who continued to develop the school. In 1601 Yagyu Sekishusai commissioned a scroll of Yagyu Shin Kage School techniques and called it *Certification in Yagyu School Techniques*.

Within that scroll there is a subsection of 8 techniques called *The Tengu Scroll*. Each technique has humans paired with Tengu. Similar to the Aisu Kage School, each technique is done with a different Tengu. These techniques place the reader in the role of the Tengu. The Tengu is the Uchidachi, the person doing the technique and the human figure is the Shidachi, the one pressing the attack. The Shidachi is typically the teacher's role in traditional Japanese martial arts. The names all end in "Bo" which can refer to either the human figure or the Tengu. It is not clear which, however I believe it to be the Tengu.

The scroll was originally published in 1601 without text, so it predates the previous scroll, however I placed this scroll after the last one to show what it looked like without the text, since they are similar.

Tengu Scroll

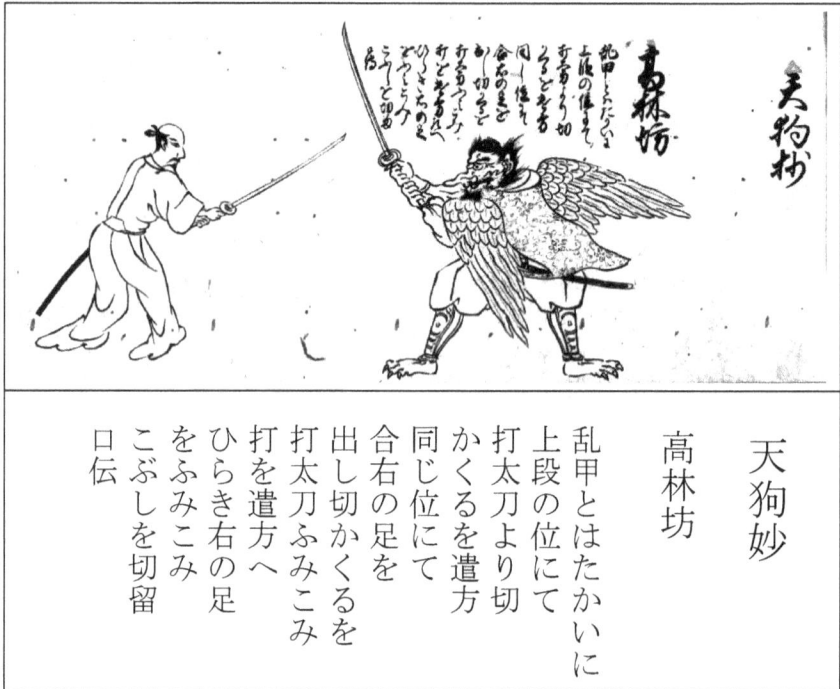

天狗妙

高林坊

乱甲とはたかいに
上段の位にて
打太刀より切
かくるを遣方
同じ位にて
合右の足を
出し切かくるを
打太刀ふみこみ
打を遣方へ
ひらき右の足
をふみこみ
こぶしを切留
口伝

Korin-bo[28] : Tall Grove Tengu
Ranko : Facing off against a violent opponent

For *Ranko*, you, the Tengu, are facing off against your attacker. You are both in Jodan upper stance. Your opponent steps forward with his right foot and attacks first. Since you are in the same stance you also step forward with your right foot, matching the attacker's right step. You then cut. For his next attack, your opponent steps towards you and cuts again. Respond by stepping out to the side. Then, step in with your right foot and finish him by cutting Kobushi, the wrist. There is a Kuden oral transmission.

---

[28] The Tengu Korin-bo resides on Mount Koya in Wakayama Prefecture. He is a guardian figure and is said to have led the Buddhist priest Kukai to the top of the mountain to meet Kariba Myojin 狩場明神. In the year 815 two Tengu, disguised as dogs, one black and one white, lead him to the top of Mount Koya.

風眼房

乗太刀とは
たがいにあや
を取打太刀
より切かけ候
を遣太刀
にてのるを
打太刀より
まきすて
引候を詰て
うてを切留
口伝

Fugen-bo : Seeing the Wind Tengu
Nori-Dachi : Riding the Sword

When doing *Riding the Sword* both you and the attacker are trying various stratagems. Your opponent attacks first. You, the Tengu, respond by lightly moving aside, as if you can float and ride the blow as it passes. Your opponent next tries to roll his sword over yours in order to wrap it up and fling it aside. He then drops back. You respond by moving in and cutting his arm.

There is a Kuden oral transmission.

太郎房

小村雲とは
打太刀より
中の青眼
にてあや
を取ふみこみ
こふしを切
所を遣方
より身
にてうら
より切
とむる
口伝

Taro-bo : Young Man Tengu
Komura-Kumo : Small Village Cloud

When doing *Small Village Cloud* ,the attacker, who is in Seigan "clear-eyed" stance moves forward and attempts various gambits to try and cut your wrist. You, the Tengu, respond by moving your body close and cutting from the right,[29] thereby stopping him. There is a Kuden oral transmission.

---

[29] The Japanese says "Ura" which can mean "from the back" but in this case means the attacker's right side.

栄意房

切詰とは
たかいに
中の
青眼
にて

を
こふし
ふみこみ
取打太刀
あやを

切を
遣方の
右方へ
ひらき
方へ
ふみこみ
こふしを
切留口伝

Ei-i-bo : Show-off Tengu
Kiri-zume : Cut and press

In *Cut and Press* both you and the attacker are in Naka no Seigan, or Clear Eyed mid-level stance. Both you and the attacker attempt various strategies and feints. The attacker comes in and tries to cut your wrist. You, the Tengu, open up to the right then step in and cut his joint, ending the duel.

There is a Kuden oral transmission.

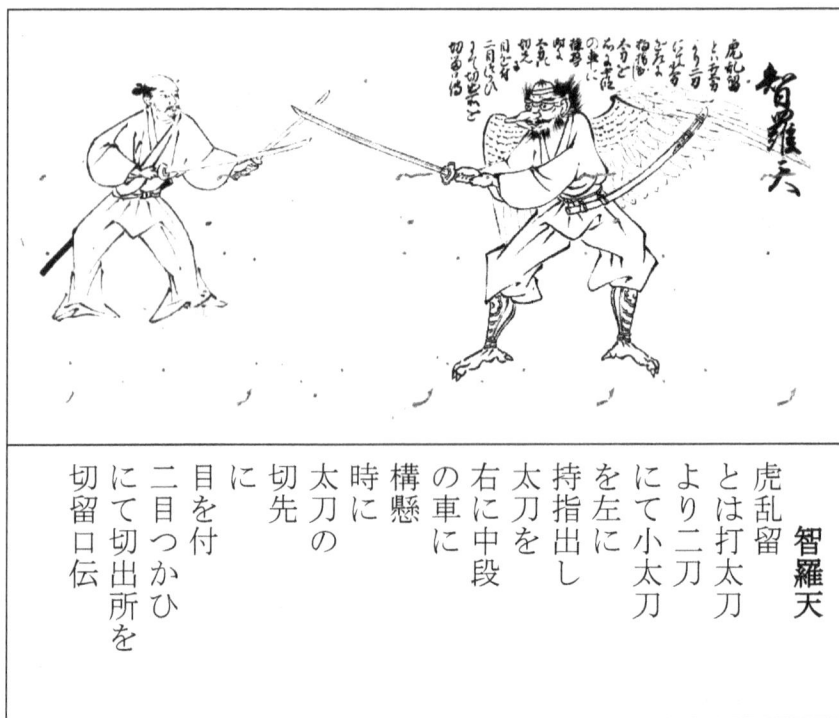

智羅天
虎乱留
とは打太刀
より二刀
にて小太刀
を左に
持指出し
太刀を
右に中段
の車に
時に
構懸
太刀の
切先
に
目を付
二目つかひ
にて切出所を
切留口伝

Chiranbo : Complete Knowledge Under Heaven
Korandome : Stopping a Wild Tiger

In *Stopping a Wild Tiger,* the attacker is using Nito, two swords. The Kodachi, or short sword, is in his left and is directed at you. His Tachi, or long sword, is in his right hand in Middle Wheel stance. The attacker will advance first.

You, the Tengu, should watch the tip of the attacker's Tachi. Use two ways of looking, and when the attacker strikes, cut and stop him.

There is a Kuden oral transmission.

火乱房

全虎乱打物
とは打太
刀より太刀
留を左に持
小太刀を
右に持
て右の
ごとく
かまへ
つる〜と
かゝる
時
身ともに
位をこぶし
を楯につき
間もなく
つるつると

かゝる先の太刀
の身へとをくな
るやうにかゝり
やう口伝
不動先に手裏剣
を切落心持いた
し候へば打出所
へ相申候。切落
にては
なく太刀
をあてがい
かゝる心持
専一也
口伝多し

Karanbo : Raging Fire Tengu
Subete Koran Uchimono-dome :
Completely Subduing the Raging Tiger

The attacker is positioned as you can see. He has his long sword in his left hand and his short sword in his right hand. The attacker begins by edging smoothly forward and then attacking. You, the Tengu, raise your sword so your hands are positioned as if you were holding a spear. The attacker will immediately move smoothly forward with his long sword. You must attack from a position even farther away than you would if you were launching the first attack. There is a Kuden oral transmission.

You should be immovable in face of the attacker's initial gambit, and maintain readiness to cut the Shuriken down. If you do so, your strike will be skillful. With regards to cutting down the Shuriken, don't think of cutting it down, rather just meeting it with your sword. There are many Kuden oral transmissions about this.

修徳房
切先詰とは
打太刀より
上段の
清眼にて
あやを
とりかゝる
時三調子
にて切先へ
つめ切
留る口伝

Shutokubo : Versed In Morality Tengu
Kisaki Zume : Suppressing the Sword Point

Suppressing the Sword Point opens with your opponent shifting from Jodan, upper stance, to Seigan, clear-eyed stance. He then attempts many strategies to draw you out. You, the Tengu, wait three beats and then move in past the tip of his sword and end the duel with a cut.

There is a Kuden oral transmission.

金比羅房
陰之霞とは
打太刀より陰の
かすみに構かゝる
時同陰の霞に
かまへ一二と合
上る時たゝと
打足を
のばし
のべの
ごとく
くはして
つめ勝。
口伝。
橋返とも
云又とう〜
切とも
申

細道
の二人
相とて
跡先
より
はさまれ
たる時も
吉と申也
口伝

Konpirabo : Mythical Water Dragon (That guards the Buddha)
Kage no Kasumi/In no Kasumi : Shadow Mist/Yin Mist

In Kage no Kasumi when opponent moves into Shadow Mist stance you also take Shadow Mist stance. Count out two beats 1, 2…then extend your striking foot forward as if you are trying to kick a Kemari ball, and close the distance thereby achieving victory. There is a Kuden oral transmission.

This is also known as Hashigaeshi, Returning Bridge as well as Toh-toh Kiri, or Cutting Through the overflow. This also describes when you find yourself in a narrow lane with a person in front of you and one behind you. This is called a Yoshi, Good Fortune. There is a Kuden oral transmission.

Translator's Note:

These eight Tengu techniques appear later in *Shin Kage Ryu Hyoho Mokuroku Koto* 新陰流兵法目録事 (1632) also known as *The Sword Master's Handbook* 兵法家伝書. The section contains 8 techniques, and while the section is called the *Tengu Scroll* the names of the techniques have been changed..

Changes to the Tengu Scroll	
1601 Certification in Yagyu Sword Art	1632 Sword Master's Handbook
高林房 Korinbo	花車 Kasha Flower Wheel
風眼房 Fugenbo	明身 Akemi Open Body
太郎坊 Tarobo	善待 Zentai Waiting Fully
栄意房 Eiibo	手引 Tebiki Entrapment
智羅房	乱剣 Ranken Wild Sword
火乱房 Karanbo	序 Jo Introduction
修徳房 Shutokubo	破 Ha Middle
金比羅房	急 Kyu Climax

Translator's Note:
Side-by-side comparison of the illustrations from 1601 & 1605

1601	1605
Korin-bo : Tall Grove Tengu	
Fugen-bo : Seeing the Wind Tengu	
Taro-bo : Young Man Tengu	
Ei-i-bo : Show-off Tengu	

Chiranbo : Complete Knowledge Under Heaven

Karanbo : Raging Fire Tengu

Shutokubo : Versed In Morality Tengu

Konpirabo : Mythical Water Dragon (That guards the Buddha)

新陰流刀法
Shinkage Ryu Toh-ho
New Shadow School Sword Method

・

1738

猿飛

一 猿飛ハ猿猴ノ身ノカロキコトヲ云千丈ノ
巌ニモトビ木末ヲ走ルニ翼アルヨリモ自
由自在ナリ此妙ヲウルハ一身ニ心満テ一
トシテ止ルコトナキ故ナリシカ云ヘトモ其
限アフンチ尋ノ谷ヲ越ント入ルニ彼ノ
岸ニ生ヒタル柳アツテ吹来ル風ノ靡ケ
ル枝ニ飛ツキテ其拍子ニ向ヘ翻ツタル
是遠キ境ニチカキ道ナリ此カシコキ
シ太刀ニ名付テ猿飛ト云ヘキ業ノ上

猿飛

一 猿飛ハ猿猴ノ身ノカロキコトヲ云テ丈ノ

巖ニモトビ木末ヲ走ルニ翼アルヨリモ自

由自在ナリ此妙ヲウルハ一身ニ心満テ一

トシテ止ルコトナキ故ナリシカ云ヘトモ其

限アランチ尋ノ谷ヲ越ントスルニ彼ノ

岸ニ生セクル柳アツテ吹来ル風ノ靡ク

ル枝ニ飛ツキテ其拍子ニ向ハ轍ワタル

是遠キ境ニチカキ道ナリ此カシコキ

ヲ太刀ニ名付テ猿飛ト云ヘキ業ノ上

Enpi
Leaping Monkey

Enpi should reflect the nimble movement of a monkey. It means your leap is strong enough to carry you to the top of a cliff 100 Jo in height. You have complete freedom of movement, beyond what is possible with wings.

If you have absorbed the essence of this technique your whole body will be full of this spirit and it will be impossible to obstruct you. Further, it is without limits allowing you to clear a bottomless chasm. You leap to the far side where willow trees grow, its branches swaying in the wind. You land on a branch, staying there for one beat before you leap easily across a vast distance. Though this span seems insurmountable barrier, it instead becomes the shortest possible route. This cleverness and deftness is the origin of the name of the sword technique Leaping Monkey.[section omitted]

名ト云ルカ何レニテモ心持ハ同ニ刀ハヘシ

法ヲ傳フト云コトアリ是ヨリ大、刀ノ

猿飛ト云ハキ一夕越絶書ニハ白猿兵

[section continues]
There is a book called *Book of the Fall of the State of Yue* has a technique called Hakuen Heiho, White Monkey Sword Technique. Understand that each of the following sword techniques derived in the same way.

Translator's note:
越絶書 Etsuzetsusho or *Book of the Fall of the State of Yue* is a Chinese military manual written in the 2nd century AD, concerning the kingdom of Yue that lasted from roughly 300~214 BC.

165

燕廻

一 燕廻ハツバメ廻ルト云コトナリ燕ハ至テ

羽ノ輕キコト何ノ鳥ヨリモ勝レタリ

喩ヘテ云ハ猛鳥一文字ニ来テ燕シ

ツカム一拍子ニ飛遠ヘテヤリスコス眼

扨ヨリモ早シコレヲ業ニメトハ猿飛

ヨリ燕廻ハ移ッテ真向ヘ切ルヲ相手

大刀ヲ横ニサ、ゲテ鎬ニ引キヲ添ヘテ

十文字ニ取搦ムシ一拍子ニ筋遠ヘテイ

Enkai
Circling Swallow

Enkai describes how a swallow flies about. The wings of a swallow are nimble and its movement is superior to all other birds. For example, if a bird of prey dives in a straight line directly at a swallow intending to seize it, at the last moment the swallow changes direction faster than you can blink your eye. When using this technique you have shifted from Leaping Monkey to Circling Swallow.

The opponent cuts straight down on top of your head. You respond by raising your sword sideways and supporting the back of the sword with your bow-hand, meaning your left hand. You are now in a Jumonji, or cross shape. You are entangled together for one moment before you slip past him.

月陰

一 月陰ハ日月陰陽トツヽキニ字トモニ極陰
ナリ月ハ形アツテ闇夜ヲ照ニ陰ハ形
ナウシテ闇夜ノ如ニ月ノ光リニ陰ヲ見
ルト云コト成ハシ譬ハ闇夜ニ戦ハヽ敵
ノ形ニ三五吾ガ影モ見ユヘカラス然ラハ
何ヲ以テ相手ニモニヤ闇キ所ニ物ヲ
ツヌルガ如ク太刀ヲ以テ地ヲ拂ツテミニ
其探ル太刀ノヒカリシ目當ニシテ戦ヘ

Gekakge
Moon and Shadow

Gekakge refers to the duality of both the sun and moon as well as Yin and Yang. Yin is dark, the moon and shadow, while Yang is the sun and light. The name of this technique takes the Kanji for moon and pairs it with the Kanji that means both Yin and Shadow. The combination has two dark elements, thus it is extreme Yang.
The moon has shape and shines, illuminating dark nights. Shadow has no shape, yet on a dark night when the moon shines, shadows can be seen.

For example, if you are fighting on a night that pitch-black, you cannot see the shape of your opponent and your shadow cannot be seen. So then, how can you engage the enemy? Just as you would call to a person in the dark, sweep the ground with your sword and use the light glinting off your searching blade as a guide to fight.

山陰

一　山陰ハ月陰ヨリ移ツテ陰陽表裏ナリ

山ハアラワレテ陽ナリ陰ハカクレテ裏也

山ニ向ツテ後口ハ廻シハ前ハウシロニナリテ

後口ハ一夕前ニ成ナリ此心持リ業ニ喩

ヘキ月陰ノ太刀下段相車ニ刀テハテ相手

ヨリ肩サキシ横ニキルトキ足リ前後

ハ蹈カユレハ肩ハシノツカラニ外レ敵ノ

後口ハ向ツテ腕ヲカヽウンテ勝ナリ敵

Yamakage
Shadow of the Mountain.

Shadow of the Mountain means you have shifted from Moon and Shadow. It represents being able to switch from Yin to Yang and Yang to Yin.

When the mountain appears before you, this is Yang, or the light. The Yang, or darkness, is hidden on the other side. If you stand facing the mountain and then move around to the back, the front of the mountain is now on the back side. At the same time the back of the mountain is now in front.

浦波

一 浦波ハ漫ミタル海上大風ニ波ノサカニキ

打テハ返ミ返シテハ打ガ如ク波ノ揉合ヲ

景色ニ業ニタトヘ山陰ノ太刀ヲ相手追

浮舟

一 浮舟ハ浦波ヨリ後ツテ波ノ懸引ニヨ

リ舟ノウク心持ヲ業ニ喩ヘテ云フヘキ

Uranami
Returning Wave

Uranami describes a turbulent sea, with waves whipped high by winds going in all directions. When two waves strike they are flung back. If flung back, they strike again. This sword technique describes how you would see the waves act in a churning sea.

Ukibune
Floating Like a Boat

We have now moved on from Uranami onto Ukibune. This technique describes the push and pull of waves and how they affect a boat. This lesson is about strategy.

Transcription from Genbun 3 (1738)
Sano Shoukyuu 佐野 勝旧

新影流

•

Shin Kage Ryu
New Shadow School
Untitled Scroll (Tengu Scroll)
1852

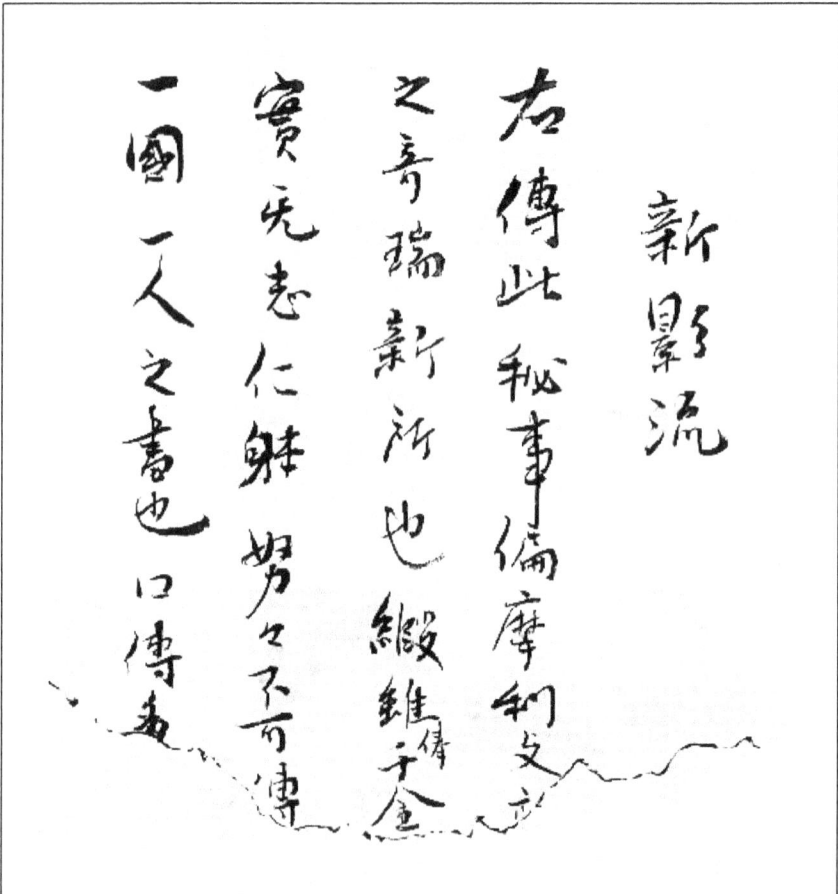

新影流

右傳此秘事偏摩利支
之奇瑞新所也緞鏈千金傳
實先志仁躰努々不可傳
一國一人之書也口傳

Shinkage Ryu

The following document contains the secret teachings of Marishiten and form the foundation of this new school. These Kuden, secret instructions, are transmitted with the understanding the recipient will train their body diligently and only pass them on to one other person.

*Some words are missing from this document

Number 1

Number 2

Number 3

Number 4

Number 5

Number 6

Number 7

Number 8

Number 9

第九

Number 10

第十

Number 11

Number 12

右真實歎之仁躰有之相
傳侯者一七日致精進以
誓氣血判可有相傳之努
努卒余莫傳之

The previous true lessons should have been deeply absorbed by your body. You have, over the past 17 days diligently trained and have taken a Keppan, blood oath vow. Be cautious about who you transmit this inheritance to.

高上 Koujou Rising Up

極意 Gokui The Ultimate

真妙剣　**Shinmyoken　True Divine Blade**

山霞 Yamakasumi Mountain Mist

獅子奮迅　Shishi Funjin Ferocious Lion

獅子奮迅

The lineage starts at Marishiten and then passes to Kamiizumi Guardian of Musashi and then Yagyu Guardian of Tajima. The line then passes to Yagyu Matsu Uemon before passing to the Ariji family. The final document was presented to Tanaka Shigeru by Ariji Masakatsu in the 5th year of Kanei (1582.)

新陰之流猿飛之目録

•

Shin Kage no Ryu Enpi no Mokuroku
New Shadow School Leaping Monkey
Record of Techniques
1865

新陰ノ流猿飛之目録

一凡猿飛ゑ於ハ表裏ゟ以文之
専趣為所有所謂五ヶせ眼意月
ゑ心之位能お能練自淺至深
秘術ヲ々々々〻

The purpose of, Enpi, or Leaping Monkey, is to use Sen no Sen (attacking first) or Go no Sen (waiting for the enemy to attack first) as well as making your opponent thinking you are doing one or the other. Making use of the Five Points is fundamental to this.

The Five points are : Sight, Spirit, Body, Hands, Feet. You must train relentlessly in these stances in order to move from a shallow to a deep understanding of these secret techniques.

猿飛 Enpi Leaping Monkey

猿飛

猿廻 Enkai Circling Monkey

猿廻

山陰 Yamakage Shadow of the Mountain

月影 Gekkage Moon and Shadow

浮舟 Ukibune Floating Boat

浮舟

浦波 Uranami Returning Wave

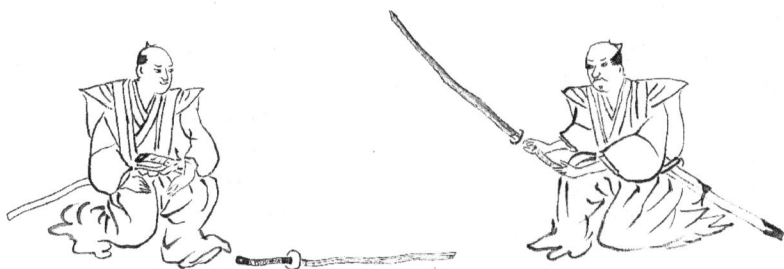

浦浪

Lineage

Udo Dai Gongen
Aisu Iko
Aisu Koshichiro
Kamiizumi
Hikida
(Lineage continues)
Yokota Risaemon

Presented to
Lord Tanaka Denkichi on March 26th of Genji 2 (1865)
(signed) Fujiwara Yoshimichi

江戸民俗史

•

History of Edo Culture and Customs
Ichikawa Masatoku
1972

安政四年の新影流猿飛の目録（伊勢守より十二人目）	慶長十五年の匹田新影流の目録（伊勢守より五人目）
 山陰	 山陰
 月影	 月影
 浮舟	 浦波
 浦波	 浮舟

199

Ansei 4 1857 *Shin Kage Ryu Mokuroku* Catalogue of Techniques New Shadow School 12 generations after Kamiizumi Ise no Kami		Keicho 15 1610 *Hikita Shin Kage Ryu Mokuroku* Catalogue of Techniques Hikita Branch of the New Shadow School 5 generations after Kamiizumi Ise no Kami	
	Yamakage		Yamakage
	Gekkage		Gekkage
	Ukibune		Uranami
	Uranami		Ukibune

倭寇と陰流

Wakou Pirates

&

The Shadow School of Sword

•

16th & 17th Century Chinese Military Manuals

Wakou Pirates & The Shadow School of Sword
16th & 17th Century Chinese Military Manuals

- Translator's Introduction

- Song of the Japanese Sword 日本刀歌
  By Ouyang Xiu 欧陽修 (1007 ~ 1072)

- 日本刀の歌 Song of the Japanese Sword
  By Tang Shun-zhi 唐順之(1507~1560)

- New Words from Guangdong 広東新語
  By Qu Dajun 屈大均 (1630 ~ 1696)

- Excerpts from: New Treatise on Military Efficiency
  By Seki Keiko 戚継光(1528~1588)

- Excerpts from: Bubishi
  By Bo Genki 茅元儀 (1594–1640)

- 異称日本伝
  Tales of the Foreign Country Known as Japan
  By Matsushita Kenrin 松下見林 (1637~ 1704)

- Excerpts from: The Japanese Pirate Sword
  By Cheng Zongyou 程宗猷 (1561-1636)

Painting of Wakou Pirates (right) fighting Ming troops (left)
倭寇図巻
16th century

Detail of the Wakou Pirates
倭寇図巻
16th century

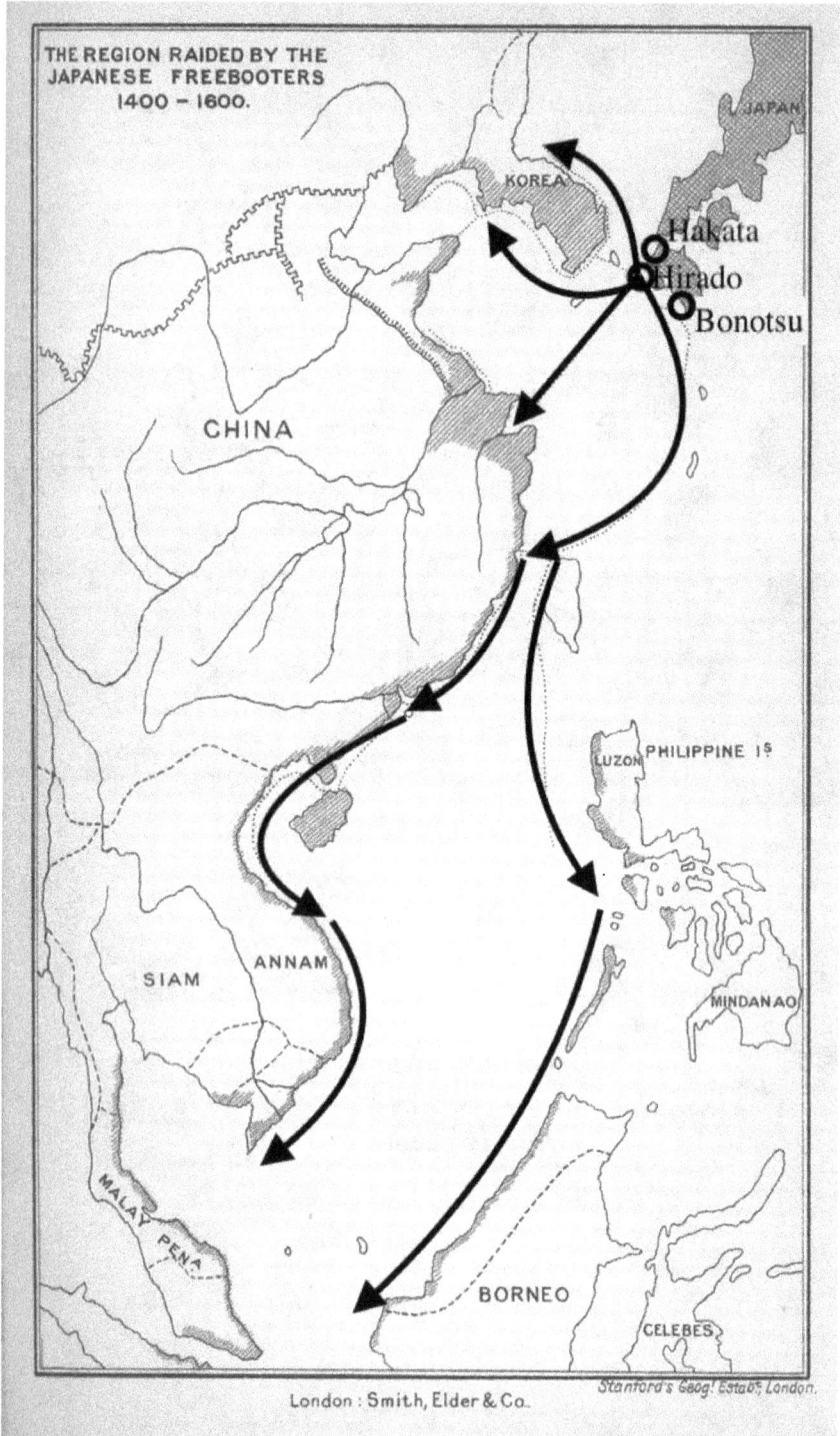

THE REGION RAIDED BY THE
JAPANESE FREEBOOTERS
1400 – 1600.

JAPAN

KOREA

Hakata
Hirado
Bonotsu

CHINA

PHILIPPINE I.S
LUZON

ANNAM
SIAM

MINDANAO

MALAY PEN.A

BORNEO
CELEBES

London : Smith, Elder & Co.

Stanford's Geog! Estab! London.

Translator's Introduction:

First Chinese Sword in Japan

Swords were first made in Japan in the Yayoi period, after the techniques were brought over from the Korean peninsula. The shape of the swords continued to evolve until a method for forging iron was developed in the middle of the Yayoi period. Trade with China began in the 3rd century AD and Chinese made swords were also imported.

First Japanese Sword in China

The first reference to a Japanese sword being brought to China was in 984. It was part of a tribute brought by the Monk Fujiwara no Chonen (938~1016.). According to the chapter titled *Japan* in *The History of Song[30]*, Fujiwara no Chonen arrived at the court of the Emperor Taizong. Chonen gave the emperor a great number of gifts including folding screens, lacquerware, inlaid boxes and an iron Katana 鐵刀[31]. This indicates that Japan had developed its sword making to a high degree and also signaled the beginning of sword exports from Japan to China.

Swords from Japan became highly regarded due to the craftsmanship of the blades as well as the fittings and scabbards.

Fame of Japanese Swords

From the 10th century onward Japanese swords as well as the scabbards and fittings had a reputation as high quality in China. In fact dozens of poets created works titled *Song of the Japanese Sword, starting with the* poet Ouyang Xiu (1007 ~ 1072.)

---

[30] The **History of Song** 宋史 is a record of the Song Dynasty (960–1279). The book is 496 chapters and includes biographies of the Song emperors as well as a record of historical events.

[31] Emperor Taizong apparently asked Chōnen many questions about Japan, eager to learn, and expressed admiration for the stability of the Japanese imperial dynasty

***Song of the Japanese Sword* 日本刀歌**
Ouyang Xiu 欧陽修 (1007 ~ 1072)

昆夷道遠不復通，世傳切玉誰能窮
寶刀近出日本國，越賈得之滄海東
魚皮裝貼香木鞘，黃白閒雜鍮與銅
百金傳入好事手，佩服可以禳妖凶
傳聞其國居大島，土壤沃饒風俗好
其先徐福詐秦民，採藥淹留丱童老
百工五種與之居，至今器玩皆精巧
前朝貢獻屢往來，士人往往工詞藻
徐福行時書未焚，逸書百篇今尚存
令嚴不許傳中國，舉世無人識古文
先王大典藏夷貊，蒼波浩蕩無通津
令人感激坐流涕，繡澀短刀何足云

日本刀歌 *Song of the Japanese Sword*
欧陽修 Ouyang Xiu (1007 ~ 1072)

The region of Kongo, where "Western Warlike People[32]" live is far and hard to reach. It is said they make swords so sharp they can cut through jade as if it were made of earth, but no one alive can say they have seen them.

Recently, the most marvelous swords have come to us from Japan. A Yue merchant acquired them from the after crossing the blue sea to the east. The scabbards are made from a fragrant wood[33], and sharkskin is attached to them. The fittings[34] are a mixture of brass, nickel and copper.

The blades are bought for a hundred pieces of gold by those who fancy them. When worn they protect the bearer from evil spirits. They originate from a great island country that has fertile lands and people with good customs and traditions.

Long ago Xu Fu[35], tricked the King of the Qin dynasty into sending him on a mission to retrieve the potion of immortality and eternal youth. He stayed over in Japan until all the young people he brought with him became old. Since he brought a hundred

---

[32] Kongo also known as Xirong in Chinese 西戎 which means "Western Warlike People." They lived on the western edges of China in 1765 ~ 1122 BC.

[33] 香木 Kohboku, scented wood, probably refers to Sandalwood or Agarwood which naturally produce a smell.

[34] This probably means the Tsuba (hand guard) and other metal pieces on the scabbard and handle.

[35] His name is 徐福 Jofuku in Japanese. He was a Chinese alchemist and explorer.(circa 255 ~ 155 BC) He served as a court sorcerer for the Quin emperor. He was sent east to find the exixer in 219 and later in 210 BC. In addition to soldiers and crew, it is said he travelled with 3,000 virgin boys and 3,000 virgin girls in addition to various craftsmen. He never returned from his second voyage. The monk Yichu wrote during the Later Zhou period (AD 951–960) that Xu Fu landed in Japan.

craftsmen of five different skills with him, that is why we have these fine blades today.

Starting in the Tang dynasty (China, 618-907) warriors frequently travelled to China and offered these blades as tribute. They were very adept at writing both literature and poetry. Since Xu Fu went to Japan before book burning was done in China[36] Thus a hundred volumes of the *Book of Documents* by Confucius can still be found there.

Due to our strict laws, copies of these books cannot be brought over to China. Thus no one in China can read these historical books written in ancient script.

Thus the revered book of our elder king (Confucius) can be found in that distant country, but we cannot cross over the great sea to get it.

Thinking of these lost books brings tears to my eyes and I find talking about my rusting short sword brings me no relief.

---

[36] The *burning of books and burying of scholars* 焚書坑儒 refers to the mass burning of texts and burying alive of nearly 500 Confucian scholars in 213 BC. The goal was to destroy philosophical books and strengthen the governments control.

日本刀歌

唐 順之

有レ客贈二我日本刀、魚鬚作レ靶青糸練二
重々碧海浮渡來、身上龍文雜二藻行一

悵然提レ刀起四顧、白日高々天迥々、
毛髮凜洌生二鷄皮一、坐失二炎蒸一日方永、
聞說倭貴初鑄成、幾藏埋藏擲二深井一、
日淘月煉火氣盡、一片凝水闘二淸冷一、
持レ此月中斫二桂樹一、顧兎應レ知避二光景一、
倭夷塗レ刀用二人血一、至レ今斑黏維能瑩、
精靈長與レ刀相隨、淸霄恍見夷鬼影、
厰來韃粗頗驕黠二、昨夜三關又聞レ警、
雖能將二此白龍沙一、奔膽一斬單于頸一、
古來神物用有レ時、且向二囊中一試二鞘韣一、

日本刀の歌 *Song of the Japanese Sword*
Tang Shun-zhi 唐順之(1507~1560)

A guest gave me a Japanese sword, the handle of it was covered with the skin of a fish and wrapped with blue thread. It floated across the deep, deep blue sea to here. The blade is covered with a dragon and intertwined with seaweed. Sadly, I raise the blade up, looking at it all over

Held up high the bright light illuminates the heavens. It causes my hair to stand on end and goosebumps to break out. When I sit the humidity is swept way as if the sun still shines.

I heard that when the Japanese barbarians first began molding swords, they would bury them in a deep well for a long time. A sword emerged only after days of quenching and months of forging, like they are battling with water frozen into a sliver of clear ice.

With such a blade you could even cut the mythical tree that grows on the moon, and the rabbit that lives there must surely flee from this glittering blade. The Japanese barbarians paint their Katana with human blood. Those who may face it should be prepared to have their blood splattered across it.

As I hold a blade infused with spiritual energy, I feel as if I am part of it. A flash of light from this blade makes night bright as day and in the blue sky I can see the shadow of the barbarian, and it looks like a devil

The Tartary nomads that dwell in the north of our country frequently display their arrogance, this night too bells rang out from three gates
Who will wield this white dragon made of iron and use it to fly up into the sky, and, with one swing, take the head of the supreme leader of the nomads?

I face the sword in its wrapping, a thing that was surely used ancient myths and legends, and begin to draw it forth.[37]

---

[37] The author of this version of *The Song of the Japanese Sword* (there are many versions by different authors) was well versed in martial arts and he may have been in battles with the Wako pirates. In addition to *The Song of the Japanese Sword* he also composed songs about spears and Kenpo fist fighting. He taught spear fighting to Seki Keiko, the author of *New Treatise on Military Efficiency* who recorded an episode about his teacher:

Tang Shun-zhi picked up a spear and taught me directly. I asked him, *When the others use their spears, they deflect the opponent's spear 5 Shaku before stabbing. However you only deflect about 1 Shaku. Why do you do it that way?*

He responded, *One-half of the human body is only about 7 or 8 Sun wide. If you deflect 1 Shaku, the opponent's spear will not touch you. By deflecting your opponent's spear far away, you are not helping yourself, only wasting energy.*

This statement is extremely enlightening to the subtleties of martial arts. Further, I asked him, *How did you learn this way of deflecting?*

His answer was, *Ten years of hard training.*

From: New Treatise on Military Efficiency 1560

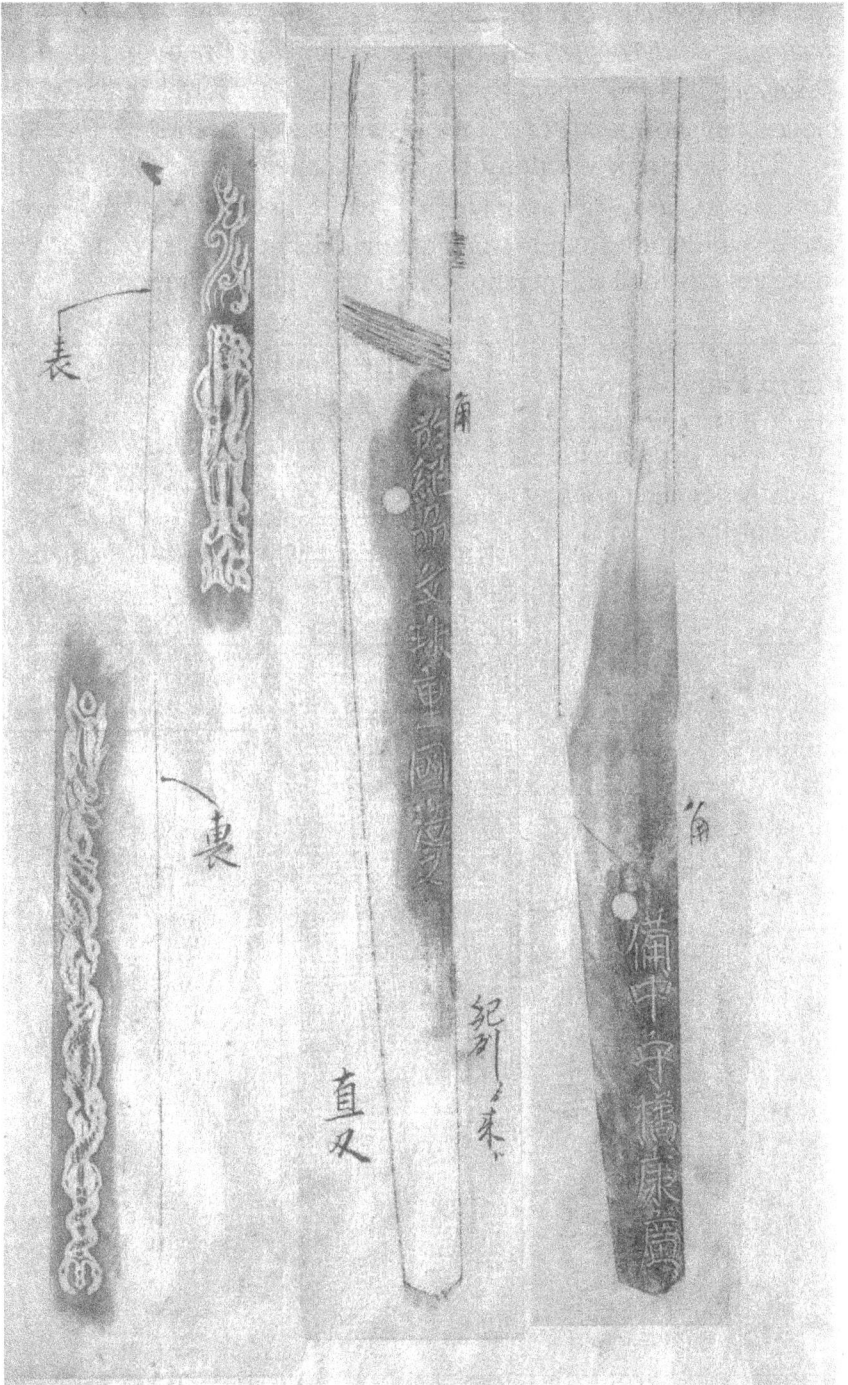

The previous poem mentioned *The blade is covered with a dragon and intertwined with seaweed.* The Edo Era book *Token Oshigata* 刀劍押形 contains some rubbings of sword handles and blades that show some of the ways swords were decorated.

This is a reproduction of a sword called *Meinankizhigeku ni Kore wo tsukuru.* It was made by Nanki Shigekuni 南紀重国 who was a swordsmith from Kishu Domain. His decedents continued to make swords for 11 generations until the Meiji restoration.

Lord Fudo Fudo is one of the Wisdom Kings. He is usually depicted holding a sword with an angry scowl.	Dragon swallowing a sword *Kurikara* 倶利伽羅 Legend has it that Fudo had to fight the representative of a different religion. Fudo transformed into the Dragon Kurikara, and wound himself around the opposing sword and started eating it from the top.

New Words from Guangdong 広東新語
Qu Dajun 屈大均 （1630～1696）

刀

羅多番刀有曰日本刀者聞其國無論國王鬼子
始生即以鑌鐵百煉淬之溪中歲凡十數煉比及

丁年催成三刀其修短以人為度長者五六尺為
上庫刀中者腰刀短小者解腕刀初冶時殺牛馬
以享刀師刀師卜日冶以毒藥入之刀成埋諸
地中月以人馬血澆之於是刀往往有神其氣色
陰晴不定每值風雨躍欲出有聲匣中鏗然其
刀惟刻上庫字者不中遠刻漢字或八幡大菩薩
單槽雙槽者澳門多之刀梅花鋼馬牙鋼為貴
刀盤有用紫銅者鏤箝金銀者燒黑金者皆作梵
書花卅有小七在刀室中調之刀奴其水上既艮
錘煅復久以故光芒炫目犀利逼人切玉若泥吹
芒斷毛髮久若發硎不折不缺其人率橫行疾鬬

New Words from Guangdong 広東新語
Qu Dajun 屈大均（1630～1696）

Translator's Introduction

Qu Dajun was famous for his vast knowledge. In the chapter titled *On Objects* in his book *New Words from Guangdong*, he wrote about Japanese Katana.

On Objects: Katana

In Guangdong, there are many foreign swords, some of which are known as Nihonto, or Japanese Katana. It is said that in that country, one hundred *hu* [a unit of capacity] are prepared from iron refined in a lake for both the tribal chiefs and the simple man, straight after birth, and every year they forge the iron several dozen times. When the man reaches adulthood, there is thus, sufficient iron to make three swords, whose lengths are decided according to the person's height. The longest is 5 or 6 Shaku and it is called Jouko 上庫"Finest Shop" Katana. The middle size is the waist sword and the shortest is the dagger.

When they begin to plan forging the swords, they kill an ox and a horse for the sword-maker to eat. Then the sword-maker chooses a day to forge the swords and he puts poison inside them. When the swords are ready, they are buried in the ground and sprinkled monthly with blood from humans and horses. Thus, the swords are imbued with spirit, their appearance depending on the climate.

On windy and rainy days, they make noises in the sheath, as if seeking to be drawn from it. The swords engraved with the characters "Jouko" are prohibited from leaving the country. In Macao, there are many swords engraved with Kanji as well as the letters of the Hachiman Daibosatsu (Sanscrit,)... Foreigners in Macao tend to carry these swords with them.[38"]

---

[38] Adapted from *The Trade in Swords and Sabers Between Macao, China and Japan* By Ma Mingda. University of Jinan. Translated from the Chinese by Zoe Copeland.

紀效新書
New Treatise on Military Efficiency

•

Kage School Catalogue
Japanese Sword
Japanese Sword Techniques
1561

Translator's Introduction

This is a translation of the portions of *New Treatise on Military Efficiency* 紀效新書 That involve Wako pirates or the Katana. This material is in volume 4 and was published in 1561. The author is Seki Keiko 戚継光, who is known in China as Qi Jiguang.

The sections covered:

● Construction of a Japanese Long Sword

● Explanation of the Japanese Long Sword

● Japanese Barbarian Training Method (Kage School Scroll)

● Japanese Training Method

● Visual Guide to Training

長刀製

粗後細爲得汰

刃長五尺後用銅護刃二尺。柄長一尺五寸共長六尺五寸重三斤八兩。

長刀解

此自倭犯中國始有之。彼以此跳舞光閃而前我兵已奪氣矣。倭善躍一迸足則丈餘刀長五尺則丈五尺兵我兵

手足篇第四

Construction of a Japanese Long Sword

From the tip of the blade to the end of the tang is 5 Shaku, 159 centimeters. Adding a handle and wrapping along with a copper Tsuba, or handguard, makes the total length of the handle 1 Shaku 5 Sun, 48 centimeters. Thus, the total length is 6 Shaku 5 Sun, or 207 centimeters[39]. It weighs 2 Kin 8 Ryo 1.7 kilograms.

Explanation of the Japanese Long Sword

Their long swords shine brightly, they leap and bound forward as if they are dancers. This destroys the spirits of our troops. The Japanese (pirates) favor this style of leaping advance. Their swords are 5 Shaku, 170 centimeters in length and we our forces are armed with short swords, standing only 1 Jo 5 Shaku, 4 meters, apart. Thus our forces are unable to meet their attack and are at a disadvantage. Though the Wato are long the pirates wield them nimbly with an excellent technique. Many of our troops are cut in half by these swords. The long swords are very sharp and since they are wielded two-handed the cuts are very powerful.

---

[39] In Japan 1 Shaku was about 30 centimeters but in China around this time the Shaku was 34 centimeters.

Japanese Barbarian Training Method (Page 1)[40]

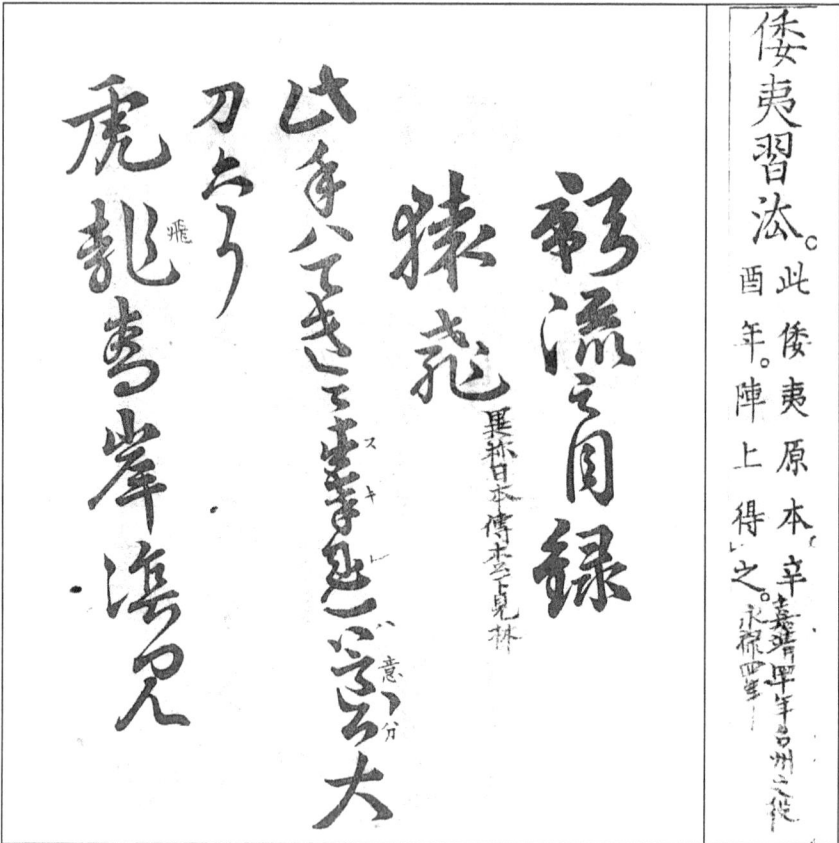

虎乱高峯瀧尺 刀ト引 此手ハてきニ圖　意ハ分　大　猿飛　異流日本傳本ニ見林　新流之目録

倭夷習汰。此倭夷原本、辛　酉年。陣上得い之。永祿四

This Japanese Barbarian Manual was aquired by our forces in 1561.

Kage Ryu Catalogue
Enpi/ Flying Monkey

　　This technique has a strong relationship to any opening the opponent may give your sword.

Totobi/Flying Tiger
Seigan/ Clear Shore
Kagemi/ Seen From the Shadow

---

[40] The Chinese engravers were not able to copy the document accurately. Thus this is a "translation" of what was inaccurately transcribed.

Japanese Barbarian Training Method (Page 2)

Further, do not allow your sword to get in sync with the opponent's sword. No matter how difficult your opponent, do not allow him to seize the initiative. This is an extremely important point. This way of fighting is known as Kokiri, or cutting off the corners. Indeed you should follow the cut of this method.
Enkai/ Circling Monkey

陰劔新書巻之四　手足篇第四　十

此ノ太刀ハ敵多ニ向ヒシ時

又太刀ノ位ヲ太刀ト合スベカラズ

時節ヲ見テ初段ノ心ヲ

以ス

牙三

小陰

This technique is for when you are facing many opponents. You should not allow your Tachi to sync with the enemy's Tachi. Seize the time that is to your advantage. Your mind should be as it was when you were at the Shodan, or low level, of swordsmanship. Third Yamakage/Shadow of the Mountain.

Japanese Training Method [41]

Mr. Watanabe believes that the reason these illustrations were changed to monkeys in the Bubishi was to reflect how Kage Ryu originated from the techniques used by monkeys. Since the Shadow School techniques are said to originate from monkeys and drawings of their shadows, the school was named Kage Ryu.

---

[41] This edition of the *New Treatise on Military Efficiency* .

End of Japanese Training Method

Visual Guide to Training #1 ~4

Visual Guide to Training # 5 ~ 8

Visual Guide to Training # 9 ~ 12

Visual Guide to Training # 13 ~ 15

Kage School Catalogue found in *New Treatise on Military Efficiency* 紀效新書 1561

3	2	1

Stance 2	Stance 1

Stance 4	Stance 3

武備志

•

Bubishi
(Treatise on Armament Technology)

- **Kage School Catalogue**

- **The Sword**

- **The Japanese Sword**

- **Japanese Sword Techniques**

1621

Translator's Introduction:

Bo Genki 茅元儀 (1594–1640) compiled the 240 chapter 武備志 *Treatise on Armament Technology* in 1621. This book was eventually made available in Japan where it is known as the Bubishi. It contains some of the same material that was include in the 1561 *New Treatise on Military Efficiency* 紀效新書.

This will be translations of the sections that relate to the Shadow School and Wakou pirates, which are in Volume #86 of the Bubishi.

- Introduction

- The Katana

- Kage School Catalogue

- The Sword

- The Japanese Sword

- Japanese Sword Techniques

The Sword

武備志卷 八十六

防風茅元儀輯

陣練制

練

教藝三

劍

茅子曰古之劍可施於戰鬪故唐太宗有劍士千
人今其法不傳斷簡殘編中有訣歌不詳其說近
有好事者得之朝鮮其勢法俱備固知中國失而
求之四裔不獨西方之等韻日本之尚書也備載
於左

武備志卷八十六 陣練制 練 教藝三

The Sword

Mao sayeth. In days long past the sword was used in battle. For that reason the Emperor Taizong of Tang (598 –649) had over one thousand sword masters. However these days the methods are not taught. There are fragments of secret poems that can be found in old documents but the explanation is not extensive.

Recently a person has done a great deed and brought it (the poem) back from Chosen (Korea). It seems that methodology is more or less complete. These techniques have been lost in China and though we have sought out copies from surrounding countries all we have found are copies written in western (old Chinese) dialects and Japanese editions of Confucius

The Katana

刀

茅子ヲ曰ク武經總要所ニ載ス刀凡テ八種而小異ナル者ハ猶ホ不

列ラ焉其ノ習法皆不傳今所ラ習フ惟タ長刀腰刀腰刀非ス

團牌ニ不用ヒ故ニ載ス於脾中ニ長刀ハ則チ倭奴ノ所ラ習世宗ノ時

進犯ス東南故ニ始テ得タリ之ヲ戚少保於ニ辛酉ノ陣上ニ得タリ其ノ習ヒ

法ヲ又タ從ヒ而演之ヲ并セ載ス於ニ後此ノ法未タ傳ノ時ニ所ラ用ル刀制

略ハ同ク但シ短ニ而重シ可ク廢ス也

武備志卷八十六、陣練制 練 教藝三 七五

The Katana

Mao sayeth. With regards to the general outline of military fundamentals there are eight major sections on Katana. I will not go into details about the minor differences. All those methods are now no longer taught. Now we are going to learn about the long Katana and the hip Katana.

The sword on the waist should not be used without the circular shield. For that reason the sword should be used together with the shield. The long Katana the weapon utilized by the Japanese pirates that attacked our southern and eastern borders throughout the Sesoshu Era of 1522-1567). That is when these techniques were first acquired (by the Chinese.)

In 1561 Commander Seki Keiko came across it from a person within his ranks and that is when this method of study was adopted. Thus it will be detailed in the following section. Before this method [with the Katana] was taught, [China] used the Katana with a similar strategy/methodology. However, as the sword used was short and heavy it should be abolished.

The Long and Short Katana

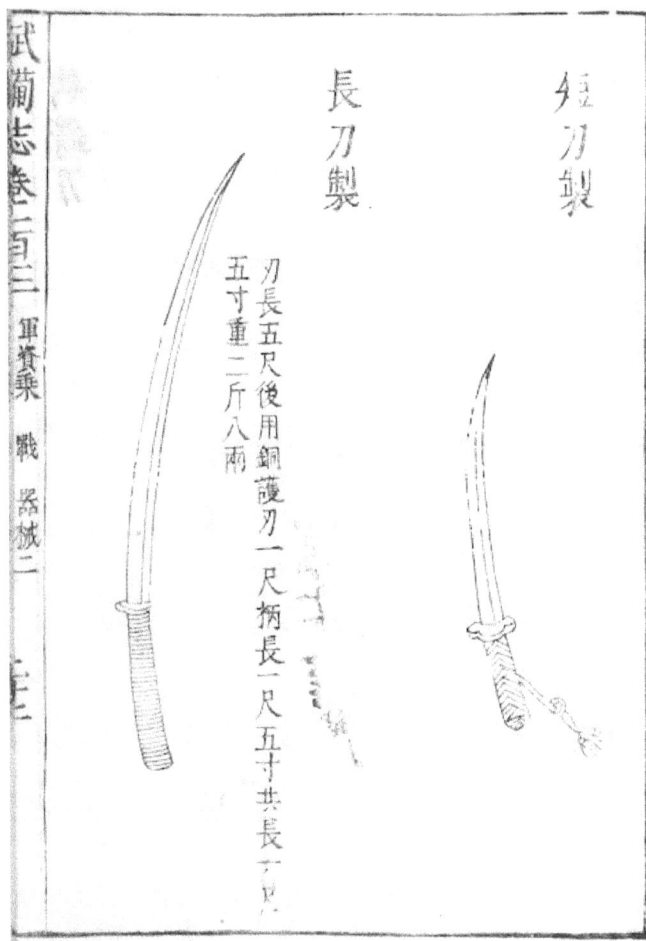

Left: Construction of the Long Katana
Right: Construction of the Short Katana

(Text on left)
Katana should be five Shaku (5ft/1.5m) in length with one Shaku (1ft/30cm) of the metal in the handle. The handle should be one Shaku five Sun in length. It should weigh two Kin and one Ryo (About 1500g).

Koshi Katana & Tsurugi
Waist Sword (left) and Chinese Style Double-Edged Swords (right)

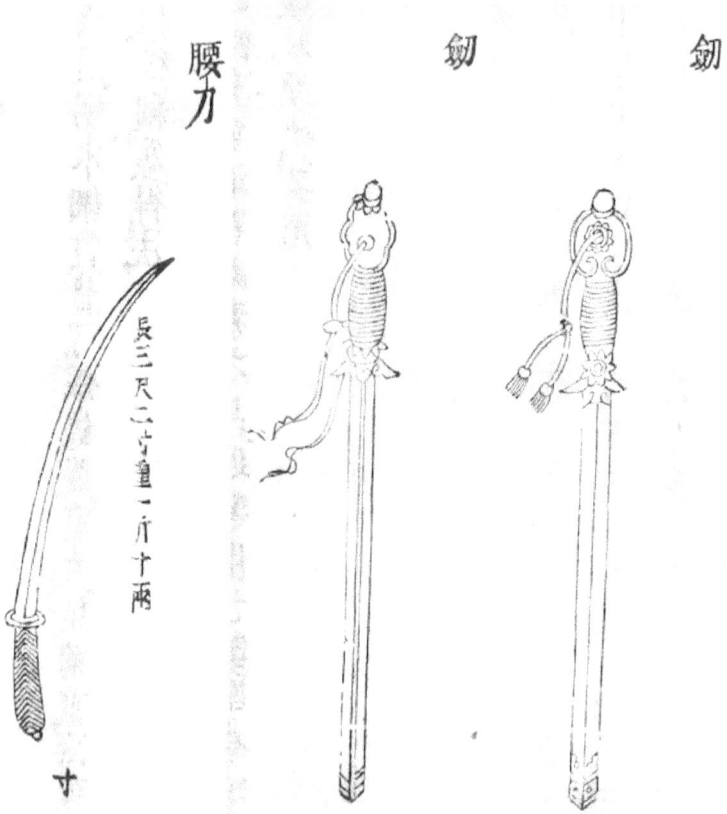

(Text on left)
Length is three Shaku and two Sun. Weight is one Kin and three Ryo.

Kage Ryu Mokuroku
Record of the Shadow School
Page 1 of 7

影流之目録

猿飛

此手ハテキニスキレハ意分
太刀タリ
虎飛青岸陰見

新流之目録

猿飛

此手ハ八さニ事態ニ宝大

刀ヲヘり

虎飛青岸陰見

Kage Ryu Catalogue
Enpi/ Flying Monkey
This technique has a strong relationship to any opening the
opponent may give your sword.
Totobi/Flying Tiger
Seigan/ Clear Shore
Kagemi/ Seen From the Shadow

Kage Ryu Mokuroku
Record of the Shadow School
Page 2 of 7

又敵ノ太刀ヲ取候ハンカ丶
リ何造作モナウ先直偏カラス
　　彼以上大事子切
ヲ意婦偏幾ナリイカ丶ニモ
　法ニキリテ有偏シ
　　　　猿回

又敵は参力せ佳く丶如
里田丶丶書きしほう丶丶丶大事
重丶書侍深筆て丶切
らくき丶高義ち丶丶大事
ほく丶うう丶丶丶丶
　　猿回

Further, do not allow your sword to get in sync with the opponent's sword. No matter how difficult your opponent, do not allow him to seize the initiative. This is an extremely important point. This way of fighting is known as Kokiri, or cutting off the corners. Indeed you should follow the cut of this method.
Enkai/ Circling Monkey

Kage Ryu Mokuroku
Record of the Shadow School
Page 3 of 7

此手モ敵多チイタス時
ワカ太刀ヲテキノ太刀ア者ス時
取偏ナリ初段ノコトク心得ヘシ
第三山陰

This technique is for when you are facing many opponents. You should not allow your Tachi to sync with the enemy's Tachi. Seize the time that is to your advantage. Your mind should be as it was when you were at the Shodan, or low level, of swordsmanship.

Third Yamakage/Shadow of the Mountain.

Kage Ryu Mokuroku
Record of the Shadow School
Page 4 of 7

Kage Ryu Mokuroku
Record of the Shadow School
Page 5 of 7

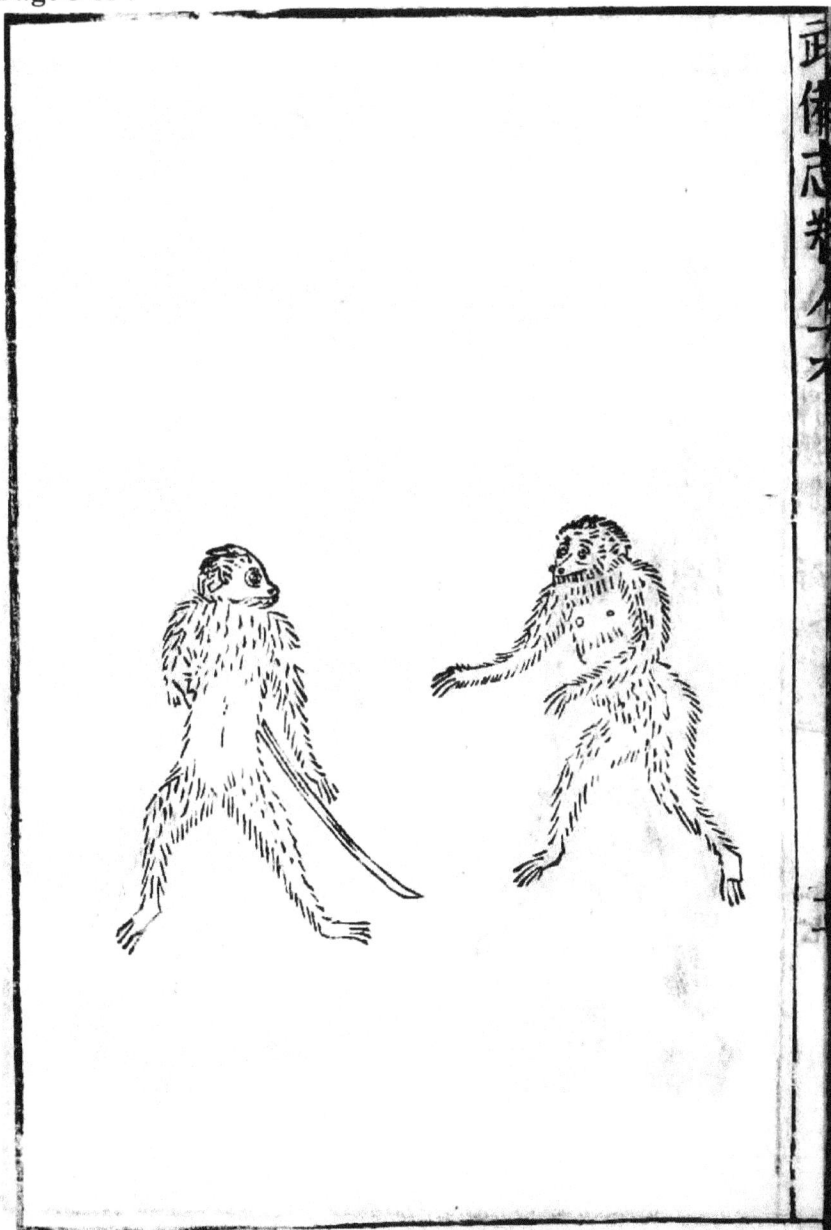

Kage Ryu Mokuroku
Record of the Shadow School
Page 6 of 7

Kage Ryu Mokuroku
Record of the Shadow School
Page 7 of 7

Training With the Katana
Page 1 of 6

Training With the Katana
Page 2 of 6

Training With the Katana
Page 4 of 6

Training With the Katana
Page 5 of 6

Training With the Katana
Page 6 of 6

	New Treatise on Military Efficiency 1561	Treatise on Armament Technology 1621
Translator's Note: Comparing the Illustrations		
1		
2		
3		
4		

AISU IKOSAI・愛洲言移香

異称日本伝

·

Tales of the Foreign Country Known as Japan
By Matsushita Kenrin 松下見林
1688

今按戚少保戚繼光辛酉明嘉靖四十七年當日本正親町

天皇永祿四年影流日本劒術者流名也影當作凡日

本自古雖多敦劒者源義經稱絕軌鞍馬寺有僧正谷寂

寞無人之境也昔權僧正壹演嘗修行佛道于此故名僧

正谷出真世傳義經少年避平治之亂到僧正谷逢異人

異人敎以劒術義經善習刺擊之法其後劒客皆多及乎

足利氏之季有日向守愛洲移香摩霜刃年入詣鵜戶權

現所業精夢神顯猿形示奧秘名著于世名家日陰流其

徒上泉武藏守藤原信綱用心損益之號新陰流有猿飛

猿回山影月影浮船浦坡覽行松風花車長短微底礁波

筆手法于氏舉猿飛猿回山陰虎飛青岸陰見之名而收

入國字傳寫之誤滸草有鐵畫

Translator's Introduction

Copies of the *Treatise on Armament Technology or* made their way to Japan where it is known as the *Bubishi*. In 1688 the historian Matsushita Kenrin 松下見林 published a book called *Tales of the Foreign Country Known as Japan* 異称日本伝 which examines primarily Chinese and Korean sources for mentions of Japan. Over the course of thirty years Matasushita collected 126 such volumes. He reproduced any passages that referred to Japan and added them to his book along with his own commentary and critique.

Matsushita acquired a copy of the Bubishi and discusses the Kage Ryu document found within it. Matsushita transcribed the Kage School document into standard Japanese.

The Japanese text reproduced by the Chinese engravers is identical in both the *New Treatise on Military Efficiency* (1561) and *Treatise on Armament Technology* (1621.) This next section translates the Chinese document as transcribed by Matsushita *Tales of the Foreign Country Known as Japan*. This is clearly riddled with transcription errors, however for several hundred years this was the only interpretation widely available.

影流之目録猿飛　此手ハテキニスキレハ意分　太タリ虎飛青岸陰見又敵ノ太刀ヲ取候ハンカヘリ何造作モナウ先直偏カラス彼以上大事子切ヲ意婦偏幾ナリイカニモ法ニキリテ有偏シ猿回此手モ敵多チイタス時ワカ太刀ヲテキノ太刀ア者ス時取偏ナリ初段ノコトク心得ヘシ第三山陰

影流之目録　猿飛　此手ハテキニスキレハ意分太刀タリ　虎飛青岸陰見　又敵ノ太刀ヲ取候ハンカヘリ何造作モナウ先直偏カラス彼以大事子切ヲ意婦偏幾ナリイカ二モ法二キリテ有偏ヘシ　猿回此手モ敵多チイタス時ワカ太刀ヲテキノ太刀ア者ス時取偏ナリ初段ノコトク心得ヘシ　第三山陰益此備志所載有欠誤大抵應如是

Complete text from the Kage Ryu Mokuroku found in Chinese Military Manuals.

影流之目録

猿飛

此手ハテキニスキレハ意分
太刀タリ
虎飛青岸陰見

又敵ノ太刀ヲ取候ハンカ、
リ何造作モナウ先直偏カラス
彼以上大事子切

ヲ意婦偏幾ナリイカ、ニモ
法ニキリテ有偏シ
猿回

此手モ敵多チイタス時
ワカ太刀ヲテキノ太刀ア者ス時
取偏ナリ初段ノコトク心得ヘシ
第三山陰

Kage Ryu Catalogue
Enpi/ Flying Monkey
This technique has a strong relationship to any opening the opponent may give and your Tachi.
Totobi/Flying Tiger
Seigan/Clear Shore
Kagemi/ Seen From the Shadow
Further, do not allow your sword to get in sync with the opponent's Tachi. No matter how difficult your opponent do not change the position of the tip of your sword. This is an extremely important point. This (way of fighting?) is known as Kokiri, or cutting off the corners. Indeed you should follow the cut of this method(?).

Enkai/ Circling Monkey
This technique is for when you are facing many opponents. You should not allow your Tachi to sync with the enemy's Tachi. Seize the time that is to your advantage. Your mind should be as it was when you were at the Shodan, or low level, of swordsmanship.
Third: Yamakage/Shadow of the Mountain.

266

The same section from the Aisu Kage Scroll 1576

愛洲陰之流目録

猿飛

此手ハ敵カヨケレハ切太
刀也又虎乱

清眼　陰剱

太刀ヲツカイテ懸ル心
少モ動顚スベカラス
以傳太事可切納ム
イカニモツョク切テ懸テ
後ヘサルヘシ

第二　猿廻

此ノ手モ敵切出ス時我太刀
ヲ敵ノ太刀ニ切續テ太刀ヲ
ハッス時切也初之如ク心
得ヘシ

第三山陰

Aisu Kage School Catalogue

猿飛 *Enpi* Leaping Monkey

If your enemy avoids or blocks your attack, respond with this cut. In addition, this technique can also be used with the following Kamae : *Koran* Wild Tiger, *Seigan* Clear Vision, *Kage Ken* Shadow Sword.

Though you are using your sword to defend, your spirit should maintain the initiative. Do not divert from or allow yourself to be diverted from this strategy.

This is an important lesson and should be thoroughly absorbed. You should take the initiative a cut forcefully then leap backwards like a monkey.

猿廻 *Enkai* Circling Monkey

Like the previous technique the attacker cuts at you. You block this with your sword. The moment the swords separate, make your cut.

山陰 *Yamakage* Shadow of the Mountain

Another section of Matsushita's *Tales of the Foreign Country Known as Japan* describes the origins of the Kage School.

今按戚少保戚繼光辛酉明嘉靖四十年當日本正親町
天皇永祿四年影流日本劍術者流名也影當作陰凡日
本自古雖多敦劍者源義經稱絕軌鞍馬寺有僧正谷寂
寞無人之境也昔權僧正壹演嘗修行佛道于此故名僧
正谷言傳世傳義經少年避平治之亂到僧正谷逢異人
言傳出真異人教以劍術義經善習劍擊之法其後劍客若多及乎
異人教以劍術義經善習劍擊之法其後劍客若多及乎
足利氏之季有日向守愛洲移香磨霜刃年入詣鵜戸權
現新業精夢神顯猿形示奧秘名著于世名家曰陰流其
徒上泉武藏守藤原信綱用心損益之號新陰流有猿飛
猿回山影月影浮船浦波覽行松風花軍長短微底礪波
等手法牟氏樂猿飛猿回山陰虎飛青岸陰見之名而收
入國字傳寫之誤務草有鈇畫

Origins of the Kage School

Now we are going to take a look at Commander Seki whose full name is Seki Keiko, known as Qi Jiguang in China. He lived in the fortieth cycle of "The Younger Brother of Metal" being beside "Bird" or Kanototori 辛酉[42]of the stems and branches cycle. In relation to Japan Seki Keiko was active during the reign of Emperor Ōgimachi (1517 ~1593.) Specifically, the fourth year of Eiroku (1561.)

Kage Ryu, or the Shadow School, is the name of a Japanese school of sword fighting. The Kanji for Kage used in this document clearly should not be 影 but 影. The Kanji 陰 is the one that represents the Yin of Yin and Yang. It goes without saying that in Japan, from times long past, swords were used extensively. That being said it was the 12th century Samurai Minamoto no Yoshitsune who attained a proficiency with the sword of unimaginable heights.

Kurama Temple is in Sojogatani, or True Monk Valley. It was a lonely depopulated environment. Long ago the high level monk Ichien (803-867) visited the temple and became enlightened to the true path of Buddhism. Thus he named the place True Monk Valley. This story is handed down in the Shingon sect of Buddhism. It is well known that when Yoshitsune was a youth fleeing the Heiji Rebellion he ended up in Sojogatani where he met a man from another land. Using the Kenjutsu he was taught by this foreign teacher he was able to fully master a method for cutting and stabbing.

From then on swordsmen from all over the country appeared. Yoshitsune's teaching were passed on generation after generation down to the Ashikaga Shogun and Asu Iko the Guardian of Hyuga. For a great number of years he *polished his sword until it shone like a blade of frost.*

Later Aisu Iko went to Udo Shrine and prayed to Kongen, the deity enshrined there divine insight into his sword technique. In his dream God, in the shape of a monkey, taught him the inner secrets of the sword arts. The names he revealed to the world. He named his school Kage Ryu. One of his disciples was Kamiizumi Fujiwara

---

[42] Japanese swords were sometimes called Kanototori Swords.

Nobutsuna The Guardian of Musashi. Kamiizumi devoted his spirit to further refining the techniques and called his school Shin Kage Ryu, The New Shadow School.

The names of the methods are Flying Monkey, Circling Monkey, Shadow of the Mountain, Moon and Shadow, Floating Like A Boat, Reverse Wave, Watching the Way, Pine Wind, Flowered Cart, Long and Short, Absolute Bottom and Waves on a Rocky Beach.

Mao Yuanyi, the man who complied *Treatise on Armament Technology*, listed the names of the techniques in this school as Flying Monkey, Circling Monkey, Shadow of the Mountain, Flying Tiger, Pure Shore and Looking at Shadows in Chinese. When copying the document it appears there were many transcription errors as well as pictures that are missing.[43]

---

[43] The line *...polished his sword until it shone like a blade of frost...* is from a book of Chinese poems from the year zero through the 13th century called *A Treasury of Old Works* 古文眞寶

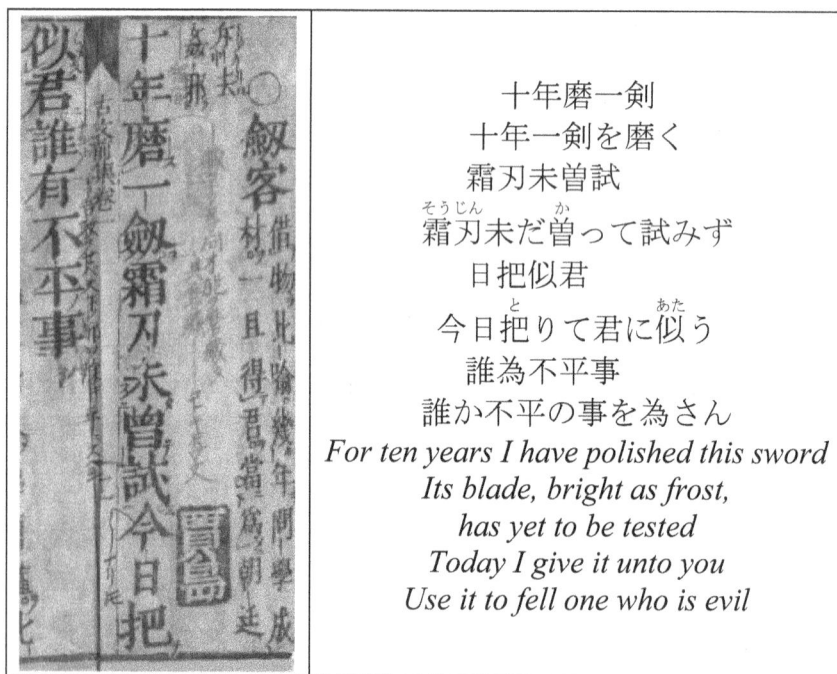

十年磨一劍
十年一劍を磨く
霜刃未曽試
霜刃未だ曽って試みず
日把似君
今日把りて君に似う
誰為不平事
誰か不平の事を為さん
For ten years I have polished this sword
Its blade, bright as frost,
has yet to be tested
Today I give it unto you
Use it to fell one who is evil

単刀法選

•

The Japanese Pirate Sword
By Cheng Zongyou 程宗猷
1614

	**單刀法選** The Japanese Pirate Sword *Selected Katana Techniques*
	**長鎗法選** *Selected Long Spear* *Techniques*
	**蹶張心法** *How to Use the Foot Drawn* *Crossbow*

Translator's Introduction

Author

The Japanese Pirate Sword was written by Cheng Zongyou, who lived 1561-1636. Cheng was the son of a wealthy merchant, however since he was interested in martial arts he decided to study at the Shaolin Temple instead of continuing the family business. Cheng studied at the Shaolin Temple for over ten years and later published several illustrated books on martial arts including Shaolin staff, spear and unarmed fighting. These were the first documents detailing Shaolin techniques, which had only been orally transmitted up to that point. Portions of Cheng's books were reproduced in the Mao Yuanyi's *Bubishi* in 1621.

About the Translation

The Japanese Pirate Sword is a translation of the Chinese book 單刀法選 read as *Dandaofa Xuan* in Chinese and *Tanto Hosen* in Japanese. Translated directly the title is *Selected Simple Sword Techniques*. The first two Kanji of the title are 單刀 "simple sword" This is one of several terms used at the time to describe the Japanese Katana, in addition to 長刀 "long sword" and 倭刀 "Japanese sword." In this case "simple" means "single edged" as opposed to the double-edged swords widely used in the Chinese military.

Since the techniques shown use the Japanese Katana, the stances are from Japanese sword fighting and the techniques are the ones used by the Wakou pirates, I chose *The Japanese Pirate Sword* as the title. In addition, the names of the techniques will be as they appear in Japanese. The book was originally published in 1614, however the edition used for this translation is part of a three book series *Skills Beyond Farming* 耕餘剩技 published by Cheng Zongyou in 1621. The books are:

蹶張心法 *How to Use the Foot Drawn Crossbow*
長鎗法選 *Selected Long Spear Techniques*
單刀法選 *The Japanese Pirate Sword (Selected Katana Techniques)*

This excerpt will consist of a translation of the introduction and 23 techniques with the Japanese sword.

The Japanese Pirate Sword
By Cheng Zongyou

單刀法選

新都程冲斗宗猷著　觀其時瀾

弟　伯誠宗信　訂　仲深時通

侯民應萬　好禹跡時淶閱

涵袥子順　德正時澤

姪君信儒家校　觀正時湏

浙江侶儕氏施昇平較梓

單刀說

罷名單刀。以雙手用一刀也。其技擅自倭奴殷煉精堅制度輕利靶鞘等物各各如法。非他方之刀可並且善磨整。光耀射目令人寒心。其用法左右跳躍奇詐詭秘人莫能測。故長技每每常敗於刀。余故訪求其法。有浙師劉雲峰者。得倭之眞傳不吝授余頗盡壺奥。時南北皆聞亳州郭

The Japanese Pirate Sword
By Cheng Zongyou
Published in 1614

単刀説
An Explanation of the Katana

The Katana is called the Tanto, Simple Sword, since it has a single blade. The Katana is used with a two-handed grip. These techniques were taken from the Japanese, who excelled at using this sword. The blade is forged hard and it is light and sharp. There are prescribed methods for crafting each part of the sword from the handle to the scabbard. No other sword can compare to this craftsmanship. Further, the glint shining off the finely polished blade pierces the eye, chilling those that face it to the bone.

Use the Katana while jumping from side to side in a secretive and deceptive fashion, meaning an opponent cannot predict your movement. Thus even opponents armed with long weapons will invariably fail when faced with this Katana technique. Therefore I sought to learn these techniques.

A man named Ryu Unho 劉雲峰 "Clouds Around the Peaks," a teacher from Sekkoh 浙江, was able to study this weapon. Ryu had received direct instruction in this weapon from a Japanese instructor. Ryu taught me all aspects of this art, without omission, until I had learned the inner mysteries[44] of the Japanese Katana.

At the time, there was a man named Kaku Gotoh "Five Swords" 郭五刀 from Hakushu 亳州 who was famous both north and south of Sekkoh province. I paid a friendly visit to him. However, when I saw the sword master Kaku "Five Swords" technique and comparted it to the sword master Ryu "Clouds Around the Peaks" technique, I found that Ryu's technique was far more refined and was clearly superior to that of Five Swords.

---

[44] The author uses Konou 壺奥 to refer to the inner mysteries. The word translates directly as "the bottom of the clay pot" but this can also refer to a hallway within the imperial palace. Therefore someplace strictly guarded.

單刀法選

五刀名後親訪之然較之劉則劉之妙又勝於郭多矣良

元受劉刀有勢有法而無名今依勢取像擬其名使習者

易於記憶其用法亦惟以身法為要儇跳超距眼快弄捷

誘而擊之驚而取之心手俱化膽識不亂方可言妙今將

八弩蒸用亦惟選數勢繪圖直述其理之可以與鎗敵者

若遇他器而此圓轉鋒利制勝又在我矣

單刀式說

古云快馬輕刀今以倭刀為式刀〔三尺 尺 範 二刀〕則長有五

尺如執輕刀一言削不得法鐵不鍊鋼輕則僥薄砍下一

刀刀口偏歪一邊為能殺人如要堅硬則刀必厚厚必重

非有力者不能用也故制法惟以刀背要厚自下至尖漸

漸薄去兩旁脊線要高起刀口要溥此即輕重得宜也鐵

278

However, while Ryu "Clouds Around the Peaks" taught me his techniques and methodology, there were no names for anything. Therefore, for this book, I have given names to these techniques according to what they represent. This will make it easier for those learning to remember the techniques.

When using the Katana, the most important thing is how you move your body. You need to make big, nimble jumps, have quick eyes, fast hands and be able to invite the enemy to strike. By then startling him you can gain the upper hand. Your mind, hands, bravery and perception will allow your sword technique to be successful. I have drawn the figures armed with both a crossbow and a Katana. I will show various stances and techniques for defense against an opponent armed with a spear. If you should chance to face other weapons then, by using the same circular movements you can deflect your opponent's sharp spearpoint and achieve victory again.

你我拔刀勢

此因刀長遇
急時難以出
鞘故以本陣
中用刀者你
拔我刀我拔
你刀而用。

単刀圖二十三勢
Illustrated Guide to 23 Katana Techniques

1
Ji-ga Batto Sei
How to Draw Each Other's Sword

Since the Katana is long it can be difficult to draw from the scabbard in an emergency. Thus, in our unit, we draw each other's swords. You will draw your partner's Katana and he will draw your Katana.

拔刀出鞘勢

左手持鞘。右
手陽持刀靶。
先拔出少許。
再用手掌托
挈刀背出離
鞘口。以左手
持靶再換右
手共持刀靶
砍殺。

2
Batto Shussho Sei
How to Draw Your Sword

Hold the Saya with your left hand, with your right hand on top of your Katana. Your right hand is in Yang, or palm up.[45] Draw your Katana slightly out of its Saya. Hold the back of the blade in the palm of your right hand and draw it all the way out of the Saya. When your Katana is completely free of your Saya, take the handle with your left hand. Then take it with your right hand and position your hands correctly on the handle. With both hands on the handle, you can now cut.

---

[45] Yang is part of Yin-Yang, called In-Yo in Japanese. Yin represents the Dark, Moon, Female as well as the left hand. Yang is the Light, Sun and Male as well as the right hand. Further, the palm down is Yin and palm up is Yang.

埋頭刀勢

此開左邊門
戶。將左邊身
體向敵餌彼
鎗劄入。以刀
橫攔開鎗斜
進右脚換左
手共持靶聽
便砍殺。

3
Maitoh Tohsei
Buried Head Sword Technique

You have your left door[46] open. The left side of your body is facing your opponent and you are inviting him to attack you with his spear. The moment he tries to pierce you, use your Katana to block his spear from the side. Step diagonally forward with your right foot and, joining your left hand to the handle, cut down as hard as you can.

---

[46] "Left Door" seems to refer to the left side of your body.

下斜撩而上。
右尖讓手自。
撩起也鎗進。
則將刁自下。
空餌彼鎗入。
門戶側身放。
此亦開左邊。
入洞刀勢

4
Nyudo Tohsei
Entering the Cave Sword Technique

Your left door is open in this stance as well. With your body facing to the side you are indicating you are vulnerable, and inviting the opponent to attack with his spear. If he attacks, then use your Katana to thrust the shaft of his spear up from below. Step forward with you right foot and cut diagonally upward from below holding your sword one-handed.

單撩刀勢

此先或立埋
頭勢或入洞
勢餌彼鎗刼
入我將刀橫
揭起開彼鎗
斜進右腳單
手自下撩起
一刀

5

Tanryoh Tohsei

One-Handed Rising Cut Technique

First of all, stand in either Buried Head Sword Stance or
Entering the Cave Sword Stance and invite your opponent to attack
with his spear. If he attacks respond by sweeping your sword across
the side of his spear, knocking it aside. Then step diagonally
forward with your right foot and cut up from below. This should be
a cut and lift.

Entering the Cave Stance	Buried Head Stance

腰砍刀勢

此先單手撩
一刀其勢力
巳歸於左邊
單手再復回
橫砍一刀

6
Yohkan Tohsei
Waist Cut Technique

First of all, cut and lift upward one-handed. When your cut is returning to the left, turn this into a one-handed horizontal cut. Use the power from that cut to bring your sword to the left, then cut again with one hand. This time you are cutting across horizontally.

右獨立刀勢

此開右邊門
戶。彼鎗劄入。
則將刀往右⊙
後⊙一攬開鎗。
斜進右步為
左獨立聽便
砍殺。

7
Migi Dokuritsu Tohsei
Right Single Leg Katana Technique

Open up the door on your right side. When your opponent stabs with his spear, swing your Katana back and to the right, knocking his spear aside.

When you step diagonally forward with your right foot, go into Left Supporting Sword Stance. Then cut down as hard as you can.

左獨立刀勢

此開左邊門
戶。彼鎗剎入
則將刀往左
後一攪開鎗
斜進右步砍
一刀。

8
Hidari Dokuritsu Tohsei
Left Single Leg Katana Technique

Open the door on your left side. When your opponent stabs with his spear, cut back and to the left to sweep his spear aside. Step diagonally forward with your right foot and cut down with your Katana.

左提撩刀勢

此亦開右邊
門戶彼鎗劄
入則將刀自
下斜撩而上
進左步復成
右提撩聽便
砍殺。乃此
技之絕也。二勢

9
Hidari Teiryo Tohsei
Left Meet and Lift Katana Technique

Open the door on your right side. If your opponent stabs with his spear, swing your Katana diagonally upward from below, striking and lifting his spear. Step forward with your left foot and you will be in Right Meet and Lift stance. Cut down as hard as you can.

The Japanese excel at these two movements and they can be very hard to defend against.

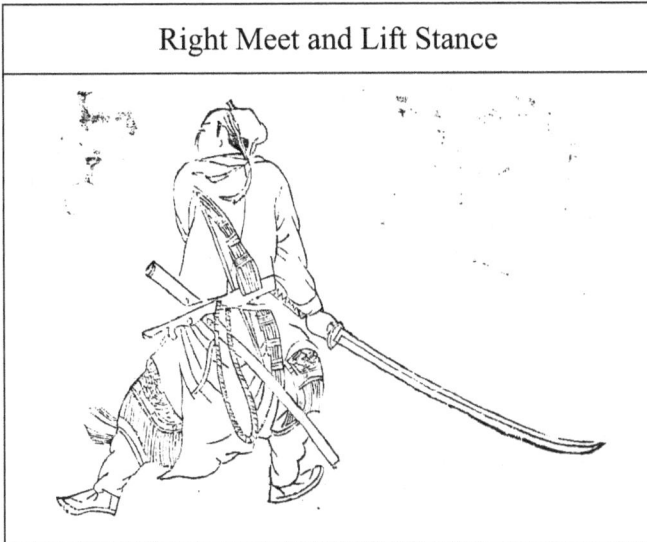

Right Meet and Lift Stance

拗步刀勢

此左腳向前、開右腳門戶，彼鎗往右後○則一刀剒入○再攬進右腳○步斜進左腳○剪砍殺。入聽便

10
Yoho Tohsei
Cross-Step Katana Technique

Stand with your left foot forward and the door on your right side open. If your opponent stabs with his spear, swing your Katana to the right and back, knocking his spear away. Step forward with your right foot and then again with your left. Take a short, quick diagonal step toward your opponent and cut down as hard as you can.

低看刀勢

此亦開右邊
門戶彼鎗劄
入則將刀往
右一格進右
妥於左邊復
成上弓勢此
二勢左右格
鎗兩邊閃躲。
進步跟鎗勿
離聽便砍殺。

11
Teikan Tohsei
Watching From Below Katana Technique

Open up your right door. If your opponent stabs with his spear, swing your sword to the right one time as you step across your left foot with your right. You are now in Upper Bow stance.

Use these two movements, Watching From Below and Upper Bow, to fend off the opponent's spear You are twisting your body first to one side, then to the other, avoiding your opponent's attacks. Advance while keeping the shaft of your opponent's spear close to you and then cut down as hard as you can.

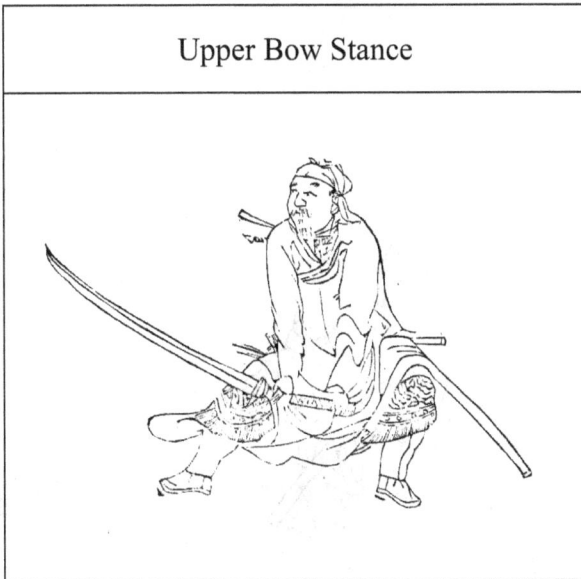

Upper Bow Stance

右提撩刀勢

此亦開左邊
門戶彼銃劏
入則將刀自
下斜撩而上
進右步則成
左提撩

12
Migi Teiryo Tohsei
Right Meet and Lift Katana Technique

Open the door on your left side. When your opponent stabs with his spear, swing your Katana diagonally upward from below, striking and lifting his spear.

Step forward with your right foot and you will be in Left Meet and Lift stance.

Left Meet and Lift Stance

外看刀勢

此開右邊門。

尸彼鎗剳入。

我進右脚

左用刀往彼鎗剳進

左脚右脚偷進

推開右脚跳橫進

步滾身

再進左脚又進

靠一刀又進一

右脚往右一

攬復砍一刀。

13
Gaikan Tohsei
Watching From the Outside Katana Technique

Open the door on your right side. When your opponent stabs with his spear, step diagonally left with your right foot and sweep his spear out to your right. Step forward with your left foot and then step forward with your right in a thief's step, so you are on the ball of your right foot. Leap up like a fountain of water. Step forward with your left foot again. Sweep your Katana to the left then step forward with your right and cut to your right. Finally cut down again.

CHENG ZONGYOU

上弓刀勢

此將刀斜橫
右膝前開當
画門戶彼鎗
剗入則將刀
往左一格進
左步於右邊
則成低看勢。

14
Jokyu Tohsei
Stringing a Bow Sword Stance

Hold your Katana diagonally in front of your right knee. Stand with your front door open. When your opponent stabs with his spear, deflect it to your left with your Katana. Step across to the right with your left foot and you end up in Watching from Below Stance.

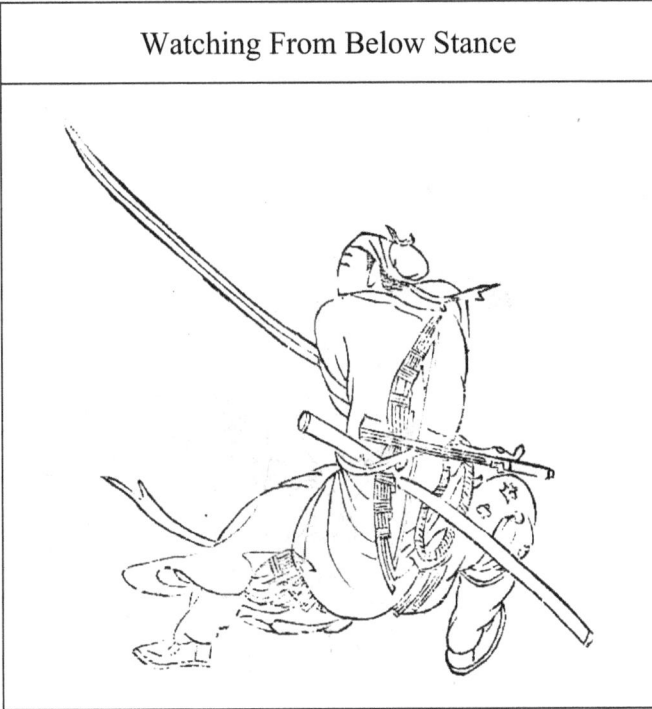

Watching From Below Stance

左定膝刀勢

將刀推出。按
於左膝上。故
鎗即有擊劈
如鎗左攔開
刀則退左步。
變成上弓勢。
如鎗右擊開
刀將身略後
一坐變成低
看勢鎗再劄
入聽便砍殺。

15
Hidari Teishitsu Tohsei
Braced on the Left Knee Katana Technique

Place the pommel of your Katana on top of your left knee, with the blade facing forward. When your opponent attacks with a spear thrust, defect it to the side or knock it down. If your opponent's spear thrust forces your Katana to the left, step back with your left foot into Stringing a Bow Stance.

If the impact of the spear on your Katana pushes you to the right, shift your weight back slightly as if you were sitting down. This mean you go into Watching From Below stance. If your opponent thrusts in with his spear again, cut down as hard as you can.

Stringing a Bow Stance	Watching From Below Stance

右定膝刀勢

此將刀推出按
右膝上如彼左
右劄我我即那
步進用刀挨削
彼鎗彼劄我腳
用刀一提彼劄
我面用刀即縊
彼挐我刀即縊
外看勢彼攔我
刀即變上弓勢。
臨更砍殺。

16
Migi Teishitsu Tohsei
Braced on the Right Knee Katana Technique

Angle your Katana out in front of you, placing the pommel on the top of your right knee. Step forward the moment the opponent stabs at you with his spear to either the left or right side of your body. Use your Katana to scrape down the shaft of his spear. If he tries to stab your legs, knock the blow downwards. If he stabs to your face, use your Katana to cut down. If your opponent deflects your Katana, shift to Watching From the Outside stance. If he blocks your Katana, shift into Stringing a Bow stance.

Stringing a Bow	Watching From the Outside

朝天刀勢

此以左肩背胯腳
向敵餌彼鎗剳入○
◎我懸起◎左腳將刀
背往左一攬開鎗○
隨進右腳砍殺○

17
Choten Tohsei
Raised to the Heavens Katana Technique

Your left shoulder as well as your back, thighs and legs should all be facing your opponent, inviting him to stab you with his spear. When he stabs, raise your left leg, sweep down to the left with the back of your Katana, thereby knocking his spear aside. Immediately step forward with your right foot and cut.

迎推刀勢

此先立外看
勢開右邊門
戶彼鎗劄不
實則將刀往
右一推開彼
鎗彼復實劄
我懷裏略偷
左腳於右砍
斷彼鎗。

18
Geisui Tohsei
Draw in and Force Out Katana Technique

First stand in Watching From the Outside Stance, with the door on your right side open. If your opponent does not make a committed attack with his spear, force it forward and to the right with your Katana.

When he commits to a strike with his spear to the center of your chest, with your left foot step slightly to the right using the thief's step, and cut his spear in half.

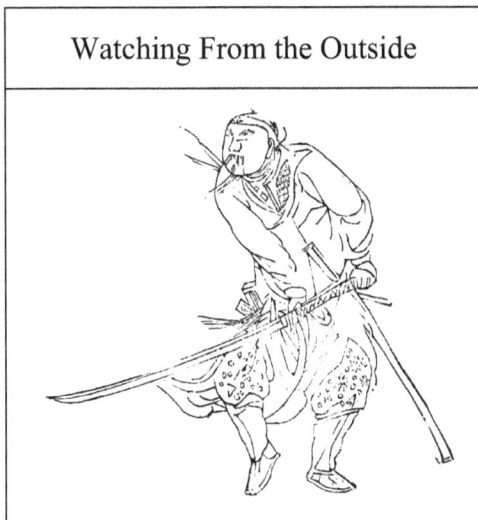

Watching From the Outside

刀背格鐵鈀勢

刀口薄始利。
如遇彼用鐵
了鐵鈀重器
之類。若將刀
口砍格則刀
口必傷。何以
殺獻故用刀
背以勢中之
法擊格為妙

19
Tohhai Kaku Tekkisei
Using the Back of your Blade to Block Iron Weapons Technique

The blade of your Katana is sharp because it is thin. If your opponent is attacking with a heavy iron polearm like a trident and you block with the blade, your Katana will invariably become damaged. You will then have trouble killing your opponent.

Thus when you are in such a situation, employ this technique that uses the back of the Katana, you will gradually become adept at the subtleties of Kobo, meaning both offense and defense.

藏刀勢

此因彼鎗變
幻難測故懸
挂小刀二三
把用一把藏
挈左手以左
肩背向敵勿
令敵見使之
無防以便將
刀飛刺

20
Zohtohsei
Stored Knife Technique

Your opponent is using his spear in an unpredictable manner, preventing you from being able to clearly see his intent. Therefore you should always have two or three knives ready.

Hold one in your left hand, as covertly as possible. Turn your left shoulder and back towards your opponent, if your opponent does not realize what you have done, it will be easy to throw a knife at him.

飛刀勢

此將小刀戒

刺去彼必招

架乘此之機

用刀砍入乃

短披長用也。

21
Hitohsei
Flying Katana Technique

When you throw your knife at him, he will invariably move to deflect it. Use that chance to move in and cut with your Katana. In other words this is a quick technique that sets you up for a full attack.

收刀入鞘勢

此先將左手

持刀靶再換

手陽掌托挈

刀背入鞘

THE JAPANESE PIRATE SWORD

22
Shutoh Nyutohsei
How to Sheathe Your Katana

First take the handle of your Katana in your left hand. Switch your hand and hold the blade with your right hand in Yang, or palm up. Then slide the Katana into your scabbard.

Timeline of Documents	
	1561 *New Treatise on Military Efficiency* 紀効新書 Seki Keiko 戚 継光
	1566 新影流 *Shin Kage Ryu* New Shadow School Document
	1576 Scroll 1-4 愛洲陰之流目録 *Aisu Kage no Ryu Mokuroku* Catalogue of Aisu Shadow School Techniques
	1601 柳生剣法許状 *Yagu Kenpo Kyojo* Certification in Yagyu Sword Art
	1605 新陰流天狗巻 *Shinkage Ryu Tengu* New Shadow School Mountain Goblin Scroll
	1605 新陰之流猿飛の目録 *Shin Kage no Ryu Enpi no Mokuroku* New Shadow School Leaping Monkey Catalogue of Techniques

1614
單刀法選
Tantohosen
The Japanese Pirate Sword
Cheng Zongyou 程宗猷

1621
武備志
Bubishi
Volume 86
Bo Genki 茅元儀

1688
異称日本伝
*Tales of the Foreign Country
Known as Japan*
Matsushita Kenrin 松下見林

1738
新陰流刀法
Shinkage Ryu Toh-ho
New Shadow School Sword
Method

	1852 新影流 *Shin Kage Ryu* New Shadow School
	1865 新陰之流猿飛之目録 *Shin Kage no Ryu Enpi no Mokuroku* New Shadow School Leaping Monkey Record of Techniques
	1972 江戸民俗史 *Edo Minzokushi* History of Edo Culture and Customs Ichikawa Masatoku

www.ingramcontent.com/pod-product-compliance
Lightning Source LLC
Chambersburg PA
CBHW050501270326
41927CB00009B/1843